MASSACRE 007

KOREAN AIR LIN

Korean Air Lines Flight 007 carrying 267 civilians from Anchorage to Seoul was shot down by a Soviet fighter on August 31 1983. The shock reverberated around the world. For hundreds of people it was a devastating personal tragedy; for millions more it was a modern nightmare come true.

Using his military experience and his skill as a successful author, Major-General Richard Rohmer analyses the inhumane and callous act and the terrifying implications of a major confrontation between two superpowers.

Massacre 007
The Story of the Korean Air Lines Flight 007

Richard Rohmer

CORONET BOOKS
Hodder and Stoughton

Copyright © 1984 by Richard Rohmer.
First published in Canada 1984 by
PaperJacks Ltd under the title
*Massacre 747: The Story of Korean
Air Lines Flight 007.*

Coronet edition 1984

British Library C.I.P.

Rohmer, Richard
  [Massacre 747]. Massacre 007.
  1. Union of Soviet Socialist Republics.
  Voenno-vozdushnye sily
  2. Korean Air Lines   3. Massacres——
  Soviet Union——History——20th century
  4. Korea (South)——History   5. Soviet Union
  ——Air defenses
  I. Title   II. Massacre 007
  957'.7   DS922.25

  ISBN 0–340–36447–5

Printed and bound in Great Britain for
Hodder and Stoughton Paperbacks, a
division of Hodder and Stoughton Ltd.,
Mill Road, Dunton Green, Sevenoaks,
Kent (Editorial Office: 47 Bedford
Square, London, WC1 3DP) by
Cox & Wyman Ltd., Reading

CONTENTS

PROLOGUE AND ACKNOWLEDGEMENTS

THE RESEARCH behind the writing of *Massacre 747* has been exhaustive. I wish to acknowledge and thank some of those who helped me with it: Dr. Christopher Bart, a professor of economics at McMaster University in Hamilton, Ontario, who has assisted me in the research of many of my books and who has become expert and resourceful at finding information; and Beverley Cline who took all the research material and organized it in such a way that I was able to get my hands on each piece of information as I required it while writing.

I am particularly indebted to Captain Charles Simpson, Vice-President of Flight Operations of Air Canada, who organized a most instructive flight from Anchorage to Seoul in the Air Canada 747 simulator in Toronto; and to the people who flew me in the simulator –Captain Don Stinson, Air Canada's Chief Pilot, B-747, Captain Howard Malone, and First Officer John Bradshaw — Second Officer Supervisor, B-747. To Captain Malone a special acknowledgement for his advice and vetting of the technical sequences. I recognize the assistance of Mr. Alan Boyd, Canadian representative on the Council of the International Civil Aviation Organization who provided me with non-classified information about the report of the ICAO investigating team.

I had hoped to fly with Korean Air Lines to Seoul and to talk with the chairman of KAL and some of the pilots who fly the R20 route. In October, KAL made a tentative offer to take me, but unfortunately did not follow through. It may well be that KAL was concerned that I might ask some difficult questions or discover some embarrassing information, particularly in the area of its cost-cutting policies and inducements to its pilots. It may well be that the airline's lawyers told it to put the stonewall up. It was certainly there.

At the time of writing this acknowledgement there is still outstanding one exciting research possibility. It is a visit to the Soviet Air Defense Forces air base at Dolinsk-Sokol on Sakhalin Island to talk with the pilot who shot down the KAL 747 and with the regional commander of the Air Defense Forces at Biya and others. I placed my request for that trip with the appropriate official at the Soviet Embassy in mid-December, telling him that I wanted to know as much as I could about the Soviet perspective in order to deal fairly with the Russian involvement.

During the first week of January 1984 a further telephone call to my contact in the Soviet Embassy disclosed that he had indeed sent a message across to Moscow in December. However, there was as yet no word. That information was encouraging because it meant that someone in Moscow was still thinking about my request. On the other hand, the reality is that the possibility of the Soviets allowing a retired air force general from "the other side" to go into one of their most sensitive military areas – one which is barred even to Soviet citizens – has to be a remote one indeed.

But the fact remains, I have not yet had a "nyet."

BOOK ONE
THE EVENT

1

THE MASSACRE OF FLIGHT 007

THE SOVIET FIGHTER pilot's voice was high-pitched with excitement and tension as he radioed to his ground control, code-named Deputat, 30,000 feet below in the darkness on Sakhalin Island.

"805. I am dropping back. Now I will try rockets."

The time was 18:23:37 GMT(Greenwich Mean Time), 3:23:37 a.m. local Japanese time.

A few seconds later he reported: "805. I am closing on the target. Am in lock-on. Distance to the target is eight kilometers (five miles)."

At 18:25:46 he spoke into his microphone again, saying two code letters "Z. G.," meaning that the warheads of the two missiles slung under the wings of his fighter were armed and ready to fire.

Alone in the twin-engined supersonic Sukhoi-15 all-weather fighter as it thundered through the frigid night air, the pilot concentrated on the image that filled the green-glowing radar screen in front of him by his left knee.

The dot in the center of the screen's sighting and aiming lines was fixed on the tail of the enormous "target" aircraft. It was eight kilometers ahead as his radar told him.

Even at that considerable distance, the target's vast wings, with its four engines hanging below them like pods, stretched from one side of the radar screen to the other.

The order from Deputat had been loud and clear when the pilot received it a few moments before: "Destroy the target."

He did not argue or protest. He would obey the order. It

was no concern of his what the identity of the target was. It could be a civilian aircraft or an American Air Force spy plane or even a bomber. It was not his responsibility to identify the intruder. His task was simply to follow the orders relayed to him by Deputat.

The Soviet pilot's eyes were glued to the radar screen with its digital "distance-to-target" numbers that decreased as his fighter gradually closed the distance to the aircraft ahead. His right hand tightly gripped the aircraft's control column thrusting up between his knees.

He was almost at the launch distance.

Now!

The thumb of his right hand pressed down hard on the two "fire" buttons at the top of the control column.

Instantly he could see a bright red glow from under the wings on each side of his fighter. The rockets had ignition. The launch was go!

The pair of ANAB missiles accelerated rapidly from their launching rails. One was infra-red heat-seeking, the other directed by its own radar. Each carried a lethal warhead of seventy pounds of high explosives.

The brilliant flame blasting from their tail pipes momentarily turned night into day around the Soviet fighter.

At 18:26:20 the Soviet pilot reported: "805. I have executed the launch."

In one second the lights of the rockets, as burning propellants thrust the missiles ever supersonically faster toward the target, had become mere pinpoints in the distance. The rockets headed unerringly for the brilliant navigation lights and the red rotating beacons of the target.

The fighter pilot knew that his heat-seeking missile, if functioning properly, would have "locked on" to one of the target's huge engines pouring out a river of intense heat into the frigid high-altitude air.

The other missile, radar-controlled, had probably locked on to the largest sector of the target, the great circular shape of the enormous fuselage. That rocket should strike the tail of the machine. The time of flight to the target should be two or three seconds.

All the Su-15 pilot could do now was watch, wait and get out of the way. He pulled back gently on the control column to gain a bit of height, perhaps two or three thousand feet.

Best to avoid any debris, because once those rockets hit the target would disintegrate. It would leave a trail of fragments, as pieces peeled off the aircraft like feathers from a bird. If the Su-15 hit even a small bit of flying metal or other material it, too, could be destroyed. So he would avoid that danger by flying a little higher while keeping an eye on the target's running lights.

It should go any moment now!

In a split second the telltale impact flames burst into a massive, billowing orange ball of fire sliced by black streaks of burning fuel. From behind and slightly above, the Soviet pilot could see the fuselage of the huge target aircraft as it was swallowed by the sphere of fire while being ripped open by the force of the simultaneous blasts of the pair of rockets; by the explosion of the instantly ignited aviation fuel in cells inside the wings above the impacted jet engine; and by the clawing pull of the air rushing out of the fuselage – decompression caused by the rockets' warheads – and by pieces of shattered engine blades penetrating the thin fuselage skin like a knife through gossamer.

A wing, severed by the rocket's explosion in the inboard engine, folded back. Then it lifted away to disappear into the darkness.

At 18:26:22 the Soviet pilot reported to Deputat: "805. The target is destroyed."

The mortally wounded 747 cut through the night sky, illuminating it for miles around. With only one wing it slowly began to roll. It was like a comet. Its long distinctive hump-like cockpit and nose thrust ahead and clear of the ball of flame as if trying to run away, to avoid being consumed. Inside the roiling fire all was being engulfed or spit out by the explosion into the icy air. Bodies were torn apart. Blankets, luggage, seats, toys – everything moveable or ripped away from the floors, ceilings and fuselage at the rear of the massive aircraft – were spewed out of the hole where the tail had been into the darkness, even before the severed tail and wing and the scorched, shattered fuselage started their separate downward paths toward the waiting blackness of the Sea of Japan almost seven miles below.

The Soviet pilot watched the results of his work in awe. This was what he had spent all his adult lifetime training to do. Defend the Motherland. That was his duty and he had done it well. He was pleased. His superiors would be pleased.

And he was satisfied not only with himself but also with his fighter pilot's knowledge that whoever was in the target aircraft had died instantly. They never knew they had been hit. There would have been no panic, no screaming, just instant, unknowing death.

Perhaps the captain and the other crew up in the flight deck ahead of the blast and flame might have survived for a few seconds. But no longer than that.

The ball of flame began to diminish rapidly as the fuselage, its single wing rolling it over and over, curved downward toward the sea.

Pilot 805 had seen enough. On top of that his fuel was running low. Time to head back to base.

At 18:26:27 he radioed: "805. I am breaking off attack."

So ended the assault against KAL Flight 007.

AS ITS disintegrated parts fell toward the Sea of Japan they left not only a trail of debris but a trail of questions that were to confound the watching, aghast free world.

A few days after the event the *New York Times* listed the unanswered questions, including the two main concerns that still remain. These were the questions listed:

– Did the Russians have any suspicions about the activities

of the plane and, if they had any, what evidence was there to support them?

- Why has the Soviet Union not offered any full account of the episode?
- Was the Korean plane crippled by electrical or other equipment failures?
- Was its radio out of operation when it was intercepted?
- If a Soviet attack seemed imminent, why did the Korean plane not call for help, using an international distress signal?

There were other basic questions at that time:

- Why did the South Korean airliner stay inside Soviet airspace for so long – almost two and a half hours?
- Why didn't the Japanese ground station warn the Korean airliner some time during those two and a half hours that it was deep in Soviet airspace?
- Was the Soviet pilot following a standard Soviet military procedure or did he receive an explicit order from high up in the Soviet military command? And how high was the source of the order? Did Yuri V. Andropov know?
- Why would the Soviet jet shoot down the plane instead of simply ordering it out of Soviet territory?
- Why did the pilot report at waypoints that he was on the proper course when in fact he was well off his flight-planned course?
- When flying in such a sensitive area shouldn't the Flight 007 crew have taken special precautions?
- Why was the Flight 007 captain so far off his flight-planned course? Was he trying a shortcut across Soviet airspace to save time and fuel? Was he on an electronic espionage mission? Was he being hijacked? Or had he made errors in feeding waypoint locations into his three Inertial Navigation Systems?
- Why didn't he monitor his weather radar, which would have shown him he was over the Kamchatka Peninsula or Sakhalin Island?
- Why are the Soviets particularly sensitive about the Kamchatka/Sakhalin region?

- Did the Soviets know that their "target" was a commercial passenger plane?
- Did the Korean plane use a transponder, an electronic identifier, which would identify it on a radar screen?
- Could the Soviets have mistaken their target for a U.S.RC-135 reconnaissance aircraft that had been in the area where Flight 007 went off course?
- Did the Soviets try to contact and warn the Korean plane?
- Did Flight 007 have its navigation and strobe lights on at the time of the attack?

Almost all of these questions have been answered.

However, there are two that remain open for informed judgment:

- If the captain of Flight 007 deliberately flew into Soviet airspace, then why was Flight 007 on that route and at that location over Soviet territory when it was shot down?
- Who in the Soviet Union gave the order to destroy Flight 007?

Those two questions will be examined in the final pages of this book. However, before the answers can be dealt with it is necessary to deal with the many facts, factors and elements that brought KAL's Boeing 747 and the Soviet Su-15 together in the night sky over Sakhalin Island. That event created the greatest single air massacre in history. It also set in motion one of the most masterful and successful propaganda campaigns in modern times.

2

NEW YORK/ANCHORAGE
TO OBLIVION

THE PASSENGERS who started to gather at Gate 15 of New York City's John F. Kennedy International Airport around ten in the evening of Tuesday, August 30, 1983, were mostly of Asian origin. That was not surprising, for the aircraft they were to board, scheduled for departure at 11:50 p.m., was Korean Air Lines Flight 007 (KE007), a Boeing 747-200B bound for Seoul, the city from which many of them had originally come to North America either as visitors or to become citizens. Among them were a substantial number of non-Asians, for the most part Americans and Canadians travelling to Korea and Japan.

Some of the gathering passengers were going on vacation or on business trips. Lee Sik Kim was on his way back to Seoul to finish his undergraduate studies, having spent the previous year attending college. Dr. Min Sik Park and his wife, Ahe Kyung Park, also a doctor – she was a clinical assistant instructor in rehabilitation medicine at the medical school of the State University of New York at Buffalo – were on their way to Korea for a two-week vacation to visit relatives. Their two young children were with them.

Larry Sayers of Stoney Creek, Ontario, was in the crowd of over two hundred passengers with their boarding passes at Gate 15. He had graduated from McMaster University in Hamilton, Ontario, with honours in English and History. When a Hong Kong girl whom he had met in university had gone back to that metropolis and found a job for him there, teaching at an Anglican girls' school, Larry had decided to join her.

There was Muriel Kole, a psychotherapist from Loudonville, New York. She was on her way to Tokyo to take part in a nutrition conference. Neil Grenfell, a director of marketing development for Eastman Kodak, and his wife, Carol Ann, were returning to Korea after a five-week vacation in the States with some business attended to at the company's head office in Rochester. Their daughters, Noelle Ann, age five, and Stacey Mary, age three, were with them.

There were several other medical doctors in the growing crowd waiting for the boarding call for Flight 007. Dr. Michael Truppin, 57, with his wife, Jan, was on his way to a Hong Kong vacation from his responsibilities as an attending physician and senior instructor at New York's Mount Sinai Hospital. From Columbia University there was Dr. Jong Jin Lim, 51, a researcher in the ophthalmology department at the College of Physicians and Surgeons. Dr. Chung Soo Yoo, 47, from the University of Pittsburgh, where he was a research chemist, was on his way to the University of Korea to conduct a one-semester course in crystallography.

Another Canadian was George Panagopoulos, 32, who was on his way to a management job at the International Hilton in Seoul. Panagopoulos had arrived in Toronto from Greece in 1973, started to work as a bus boy and wound up as assistant manager of the Toronto Harbour Castle Hilton's Poseidon Room, a restaurant. His new post in Seoul was to be a step up in the Hilton management ladder.

After the boarding announcement was made, one of the Americans to move down the boarding ramp with the throng of other passengers was Congressman Larry McDonald who had been booked on Flight 007 for the previous Sunday. Unfortunately, McDonald had missed the flight because thunderstorms in the New York area meant that his aircraft into Kennedy from Atlanta that day had to be diverted. There was a Pan American flight to Seoul that he could have taken on the Sunday, but because of the much lower KAL fare he decided to wait for the Tuesday night departure. Representative Lawrence Patton McDonald, 48, a physician from Marietta, Georgia, and a Georgia Democrat re-knowned as the most conservative member of Congress and as national chairman of the ultra-conservative John Birch Society, was on his way to South Korea. He was a member of a six-man congressional delegation representing the United States at a conference there to commemorate the thirtieth anniversary of the mutual-defense treaty between South Korea and the U.S.A. The five other members, including North Carolina Senator Jesse Helms; Idaho Senator Steve Symms and Kentucky Congressman Carroll Hubbard, would take KAL Flight 015 from Los Angeles. Hubbard had originally planned to be with McDonald on Flight 007, but the chance of a speaking engagement in Kentucky had caused him to cancel at the last minute and switch to Flight 015. Like most of the other passengers, McDonald was not looking forward to the long, grinding flight even though he had the reputation of having no trouble sleeping on planes.

So it was a mixed bag of humanity that boarded Flight 007 shortly after 11:00 on the night of August 30: children, doctors, mothers, fathers, businessmen, tradesmen, teachers, executives, and one young man, Inho Lee, 23, of Jersey City, who was going back to Korea to look for a bride.

As the passengers were getting their hand baggage stored under seats or in overhead compartments and going through the routine of settling themselves into their seats, and while the eighteen-person cabin crew were receiving and directing passengers or carrying out pre-takeoff tasks in the galleys, the aircraft's captain, Taek Yong Choi, and his co-pilot and engineer were busily engaged in the 747's cockpit. With meticulous care, they were going through their pre-start and pre-flight checks. One of the most important procedures they would follow – and this had to be done when the aircraft was stationary – was to punch in on the Inertial Navigation System (INS) keyboard (Figure 2:1) the precise latitude and

20

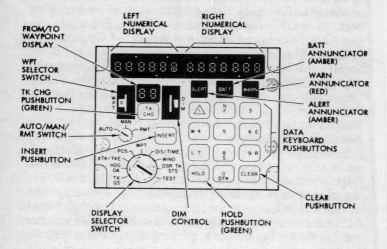

Figure 2:1 Inertial Navigation System Control/Display Unit. (For the location of all three INS, see the picture of the Boeing 747 cockpit in photo section.)

longitude of each compulsory reporting point (waypoint) on the route from New York across American and Canadian airspace to Anchorage. The pilots would load into the INS a maximum of nine position points, plus the present position (ramp) point, the exact latitude and longitude of their ramp spot at Kennedy International Airport. It would go in first – while the aircraft was stationary – inserted by the co-pilot and checked by the captain and the flight engineer. Then the rest would be inserted, the last one of the nine being a waypoint well into the trip. The latitude and longitude of Anchorage would be fed into the INS during the flight after sufficient progressive waypoint passages had been made to allow the destination to be inserted. The route that the pilots would follow was on a computer printout of the flight plan and also on a standard en-route map from which they would read the latitude and longitude numbers.

As the co-pilot punched the numbers into the INS they instantly appeared as glowing yellow digits on the face of the screen across the top of the INS keyboard itself. He used the "remote" system, which meant that as he fed all of the position points into the INS in front of him, those points would automatically be fed to the INS system on the captain's side and to the third one located between the two pilots' seats immediately behind the engine throttles. It would then be up to the captain to do his check of the numbers that the co-pilot had fed into the INS system to ensure that they were correct (see photo of Boeing 747 cockpit).

It was an elaborate, time-consuming process, but it had to be done absolutely correctly. There could be no errors. If there were, then the reliable INS systems, all three of them, could end up navigating the airplane to the wrong place. After all, an Inertial Navigation System, like any other computer mechanism, can only deal with the information a human has fed into it. Garbage in means garbage out, as the saying goes.

When all the checks had been completed and the ramp and waypoint information had been put into the INS and checked against the computerized flight plan, Captain Taek received radio advice that his start-up and departure would be delayed approximately thirty minutes.

Departure clearance was received at about 12:15 a.m. Captain Taek with his co-pilot and engineer began their start procedures. Their hands moved from switch to switch. Checks were called to one another. The start levers were set and the four powerful engines were started. The floodlights of the airport glinted off the shining white 747's blue and red trim. The aircraft's logo lights illuminated the fin, shining on the Korean Air Lines symbol, an encircled stylized red bird flying forward on the jumbo jet's lofting, eight-story-high tail. The great airplane was ready to move away from the two umbilical-cord doors of Gate 15. The captain gave the intercom clearance to the tractor crew to push the 747 out and away from the gate.

When the squat tractor that had pushed Flight 007 back

was detached and out of the way, Captain Taek moved the four engine throttles forward together in unison. When he did so, the passengers and crew heard and felt a deep rumbling roar as the engines produced sufficient power to get the massive airplane taxiing to Runway 31L (the left of two runways, each with a heading of 310 degrees magnetic).

At 12:23, in the darkness of New York, his takeoff clearance received and his aircraft's landing lights blazing, navigation lights shining steadily and red warning beacons flashing, Captain Taek rolled his aircraft onto the button of Runway 31L. He turned it until the machine was lined up exactly dead center between the strings of lights converging in the distance on each side of the runway.

The grip of his right hand on the throttles was confirmed by the left hand of the engineer from behind. The captain shoved the throttles slowly, positively forward, up to full power. Like a lumbering elephant, Flight 007 began to move down Runway 31L, accelerating rapidly toward the computer pre-calculated speed at which the co-pilot would call for rotation. When the rotation call came, the captain, both hands now on the wheel on the control column, hauled back smoothly and strongly. Instantly the nose came up into the climb position and the enormous aircraft, 196 feet between its blinking wing-tip lights and 232 feet between nose and tail, leapt gracefully up into the black night. It was 12:24 on the morning of September 1.

Ahead of the 244 passengers (including a family of four who would get off at Anchorage), was a grueling seven-hour, 3,400-mile flight, almost all of which would be in darkness. After a refueling break at Anchorage, the passengers would be confronted with another confining seven-and-a-half hours before they were to land at Seoul's Kimpo Airport shortly after six in the morning, local Korea time.

A few minutes after lift-off into the cloudless night, the co-pilot turned off the seat-belt sign. A short time later, with the desired altitude of 35,000 feet set on the altitude-selector unit, the captain turned the appropriate switches on the instrument panel to put the aircraft under the control of the autopilot coupled with the one INS (of the three) that would navigate.

Left to its own devices, the aircraft would now fly itself directly to Anchorage via the programmed waypoints. The 747 would even land itself automatically there if the captain chose to give the INS and other instruments the proper instructions.

When the seat-belt signs went off, the flight attendants, in their trim blue uniforms, began to move around their assigned cabins ensuring the comfort of their passengers and preparing to serve food and drink. In the upper deck lounge, immediately behind the 747's cockpit that humps out at the top of the fuselage near the nose, there were twelve first-class passengers; each of them had paid, for the round trip, $3,588.00. Before takeoff and after, champagne and wines were offered. During the long flight, the occupants of these spacious, comfortable seats would be served the finest of foods and liqueurs.

Down the circular steps below them in the twenty-four-seat "Prestige Class" section, nearly all the seats were filled by people who had paid $2,380 for the round trip and for service almost (but not quite) as good as that in the first-class section.

To the rear of Prestige Class was the economy section where passengers could fly from New York to Seoul and return for as little as $1,200. Korean Air Lines was famous for its low prices. Throughout the airline industry KAL's ultra-cheap fares meant only one thing – that the airline, in order to survive, would have to cut corners wherever it could: fuel, time in the air, ground and maintenance staff, that sort of thing. Every cost-cutting device its expert managers could lay their hands on would have to be used, perhaps even incentives for those flight-deck crews, managers and others who could shave and pare costs.

The cabin crew served drinks and snacks. Some passengers, shoes off, loosened their neckwear. Many slept. A few watched the in-flight movie, others read. The cabin lights were kept low.

Still in the darkness, Flight 007 touched down at Anchorage at 2:30 a.m. local time.

The flight to Anchorage was not totally routine for Captain

Taek. He had experienced a minor radio-reception problem. This he reported to the ground technicians as soon as he arrived. Some adjustments were made and the radios were pronounced to be serviceable.

After the aircraft came to a stop at the terminal and it was announced that passengers could disembark, most of them did just that. They left their hand luggage on the aircraft, slipped on jackets or sweaters for protection against the chill night air and, weary and bleary-eyed, made their way to the aircraft's doors and the steps down to the tarmac. In the terminal they walked about, sat, some smoked, sipped on coffee and generally stretched their legs in preparation for the long exhausting flight into Seoul.

On the other hand, some of the passengers who were easy sleepers – like Larry McDonald – decided to stay on the aircraft and do exactly that, sleep. Even the full cabin lights didn't disturb them, nor did the clean-up crews that worked through the 747's cabins. The crews made quite a racket, running vacuum cleaners at full scream, rattling ashtrays as they emptied them, picking up old newspapers, used napkins and other debris, cleaning toilets and, with much clattering and banging, restocking the galleys and bars.

Through it all, Larry McDonald slept instead of getting off. The result was that he missed seeing his colleagues, Jesse Helms, Steve Symms and Carroll Hubbard, whose KAL Flight 015 (an identical Boeing 747) arrived in Anchorage about fifteen minutes after Flight 007. They looked for McDonald in the terminal lounge and were disappointed not to find him. Helms later speculated, "Maybe if we had, we would have persuaded him to join us – or he might have got us to join him."

The call came to reboard Flight 007 just after 3:30 a.m., Anchorage time. By then there had been two important additions to the aircraft. The first was that 37,750 gallons of highly combustible jet fuel had been pumped into the aircraft's tanks, much of it sitting in wing fuel cells immediately above the four engines. There was sufficient to accommodate the 747's 6,000-mile cruising range, which would take it to

Seoul with a more than adequate reserve flying time beyond that.

The other addition was a fresh flight crew: Captain Chun Byung In, his co-pilot, Sohn Dong Hui, and the flight engineer, Kim Eui Dong. These three replaced the crew that had flown Flight 007 in from New York. Some of Captain Taek's flight-attendant crew would continue on to Seoul merely as passengers, the usual custom when crews were switched at Anchorage. Captain Taek and his co-pilot and engineer would not go on.

Captain Chun (see photo section), 45, was one of Korean Air Lines' most highly experienced and respected pilots. He had joined KAL in 1972 after serving for several years in the South Korean Air Force, the beginning place of most of KAL's pilots. With more than 10,600 flying hours as a pilot, he had 6,618 on Boeing 747's. A mark of his capability and prestige was that he was chosen to fly South Korea's president and other dignitaries during the 1983 visit to the United States. Chun was known as a strong-willed man who wanted to control other people, a man who was unlikely to negotiate. It was said that he was likely either to persuade his enemies or to force them. A relatively tall and athletic man, he kept himself flying-fit. He held a black belt in Tae Kwon Do, the martial art that is the Korean national sport. In the air force he had acquired a reputation for boldness and aggressiveness. Those characteristics and the willingness to take a chance are among the hallmarks of the highly disciplined and trained Korean Air Force.

His co-pilot, Mr. Sohn, slightly older than Chun at 47, was also a South Korean Air Force veteran who had left the service in 1977 with the rank of Lieutenant-Colonel. He joined KAL in 1979. Mr. Sohn had over 8,900 flying hours, of which some 3,441 were on 747's.

The two men had flown the run between Anchorage and Seoul dozens of times. Chun knew it "like the back of his hand." He was familiar with every aspect of the route, from Anchorage to Bethel, down the R20 route over the Pacific just east of the Soviet Union's Kamchatka Peninsula and

Kuril Islands, over the turning point, Matsushima, on the main Japanese island of Honshu, then west to Seoul.

This was the most dangerous of all routes, as Chun and his co-pilot well knew. The Soviets were extremely sensitive to any intrusion, because of the strategic military, naval and rocket installations in the region. Early warning radar systems and long-range Soviet missile-testing facilities are located on Kamchatka. Its major naval port of Petropavlovsk is the base of at least eighty nuclear-powered submarines and scores of diesel-powered undersea craft. The tip of Sakhalin Island is only twenty-seven miles from Japan's Hokkaido Island across the choke point Strait of Soya through which Soviet naval vessels must move when transiting from the Sea of Japan into the north Pacific. Close to nine hundred ships of the Soviet's Pacific fleet have as their bases Sovetskaya-Gavan and the port that gained fame during World War II, Vladivostok. The militarily oriented Captain Chun knew the dangers in that area. Furthermore, he was well-aware of the blue-lined warnings printed on his navigation charts over Kamchatka, the Sea of Okhotsk and Sakhalin Island. The words were clear: "Warning: Aircraft infringing upon Non-Free Flying Territory may be fired on without warning."

That warning was deadly serious. U.S. RC-135 reconnaissance planes that constantly electronically monitor the Russian missile, naval and military activity in the area frequently come so close to what Soviets consider to be their airspace in the Kamchatka/Kuril area that the Soviets reportedly have fired more than a hundred surface-to-air missiles at the big reconnaissance aircraft. Their score is an amazing zero.

As the passengers were reboarding Flight 007 and settling themselves back into their seats for the long flight ahead, the new captain and his flight-deck crew were going through exactly the same pre-start checks and procedures that Captain Taek's team had carried out in New York many hours earlier.

It was time to feed the waypoint co-ordinates into the

Inertial Navigation System. With great care, co-pilot Sohn began the procedure under the watchful eyes of Captain Chun and the flight engineer. First the co-ordinates for the present position (ramp) went in. Chun and the flight engineer were required to confirm these numbers by company rules.

The first waypoint, 346 nautical miles to the west, was Bethel (see Map 2:1).

Nabie was the second set of co-ordinates, 312 miles west of Bethel on a track of 239 degrees.

Then on to Neeva, a distance of 593 miles; Neeva to Nippi 561 NM; Nippi to Nokka 660 NM; and from Nokka to Noho to Inkfish to Matsushima. The co-ordinates of Kimpo Airport and the three waypoints between it and Matsushima would be inserted probably before reaching Noho. The overall distance from Anchorage to Seoul along route R20 was 3,566 NM.

Co-pilot Sohn could have fed the co-ordinates that he had just put into his own INS directly into the other two INS machines by using the "remote" system. Or he could have elected to independently insert the co-ordinates into the INS in front of him. That would have meant that the engineer would have had to do the same independently, as would the captain.

If Captain Chun had decided to fly direct to Seoul by the Great Circle Route, cutting across the Kamchatka Peninsula and Sakhalin Island, this is the moment when the final decision would have been made to do it.

IF THE TRACK Flight 007 followed, as claimed by the Russians, was correct, then the point at which Chun would have left route R20 was at its very beginning, as soon as he left Anchorage.

Since Bethel is 346 nautical miles west of Anchorage and the radar coverage of the FAA (Federal Aviation Authority) at Anchorage is only 165 nautical miles, Chun would know that at Bethel he would be beyond the checking radar operator's eyes at Anchorage and therefore free to pick up

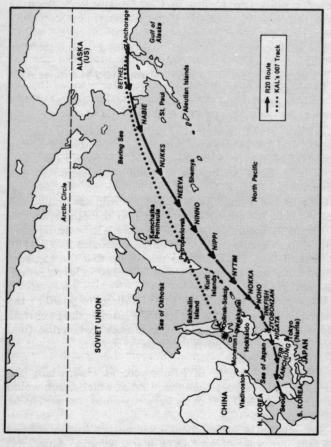

Map 2:1 R20 Route and KE 007 track.

the direct-to-Seoul track. He might be seen by U.S. military radar, but there was little or no co-ordination between the U.S. military and civil authorities.

If, for whatever reason, Chun did elect to go direct from Bethel to Seoul across Kamchatka/Sakhalin, the procedure he would have followed sitting on the ground at Anchorage would have been this:
- Chun would have punched into his own INS the co-ordinates for the ramp position and Seoul;
- his co-pilot, Sohn, would have punched into his INS the correct co-ordinates for the ramp and the nine waypoints to Bethel and along route R20 to Matsushima.

When airborne, the aircraft automatic pilot would have then been locked onto Captain Chun's INS, and would have flown the course it directed. At the same time, co-pilot Sohn's INS would be duly monitoring the distance travelled and the track error, and would be reporting to him when the aircraft was about to reach the north-south line, the longitudes of the waypoints that he had punched into the INS. When the aircraft was two minutes away from an inserted waypoint, a small amber alert light on the INS control box would come on. The co-pilot would then prepare to radio a position report to the responsible air controllers. Thus, if Captain Chun had selected the direct route from Anchorage to Seoul on his own INS, co-pilot Sohn would monitor the amber alert light, which would come on (as a function of distance) two minutes before the aircraft should be arriving at the longitude position he had punched into his own INS. That light would come on at approximately the correct time and longitude position even though the aircraft might be a hundred, or two hundred, or, as Flight 007 was when it was shot down, three hundred miles north of the correct imaginary waypoint position Sohn had originally inserted into his INS. Sohn would then pass a position report to the appropriate American or Japanese air controllers, telling them that he was over the correct check point, Neeva or Nippi or Nokka, when in fact he was, and knew that he was, many miles to the north of that point.

ON THE GROUND at Anchorage, Alaska, at approximately 3:30 a.m., local time, the flight-deck crew of Flight 007 completed the insertion of their waypoint information and directions into their three INS systems. All the pre-start checks were completed. As Flight 007 was being pushed out from the ramp, Chun and his crew fired up the jumbo's four engines and headed for departure runway 32.

Still in the darkness at 4:00 a.m., Anchorage time (13:00 GMT), Captain Chun pulled back on his control column, lifting his 747 smoothly off the runway. When the landing gear was up, the flaps retracted and the engine power set for climb, he selected autopilot and INS and released the wheel. Immediately, while still climbing toward the preset flight-planned altitude of 30,000 feet, the aircraft turned slightly to the right to pick up the heading, toward Bethel but slightly to the north of it on jet route 501. In less than half an hour's time Flight 007 would be out of Anchorage radar range.

While the huge 747 moved ever higher into the increasingly frigid high-altitude air, the cabin crew were busy at their usual task of serving their passengers. The women flight attendants now had on their native Korean dress instead of the trim blue uniforms. They wore the multi-hued chima (long skirt) and the chogori (blouse). For the tourist cabin there was orange juice and sandwiches and for the other classes, soba, a Japanese broth, cheddar and rice croquettes, zucchini au gratin, chicken florentine and other delights.

As the 747 leveled off and was approaching Bethel approximately fifty minutes into its flight, the lights had been turned down and most of the passengers were sleeping under blankets, their seat backs canted to the rear as far as possible. There was no sound except the hissing muted roar of the engines and the air rushing by the fuselage. The noise was constant and soporific.

Up in the cockpit, darkened except for the glow of the instrument lights, the co-pilot watched the INS box's amber alert light come on. Two minutes to the Bethel waypoint passage. At the waypoint the amber light went on. The co-pilot would make a report to Anchorage at this waypoint even though it was not a compulsory reporting location. The first compulsory waypoint west of Anchorage on route R20 would be at Nabie, 658 nautical miles into the flight.

Bethel was the critical point. If Chun had deliberately programmed his own INS to go direct to Seoul, he would pass about 12 NM north of the Bethel VOR (VHF omni-directional range – a powerful radio beacon). Even if he had not done so, but there was some mistake or error in the insertion of the ramp co-ordinates or in the handling of the INS controls and switches, it was before Bethel that the movement of Flight 007 along a track to the north and right of R20 began. That course would take it over or near Petropavlovsk and across Sakhalin Island. The track it would take would be almost exactly the Great Circle Route from Anchorage to Seoul.

About one hour past Bethel, the pilots noticed that the radar-sensing-indicator blue light on the transponder panel just behind the throttles was glowing. That light indicated that some radar set somewhere was bouncing its signals off the 747. Was it the Soviet radar net on Kamchatka or was it an American military radar installation somewhere in the Aleutians? Either way, it was not an unusual situation for Flight 007 to be under radar surveillance on R20. The reality of Flight 007's track was that at that point it was approximately one hundred miles off the Kamchatka coast heading for the Petropavlovsk area about five hundred nautical miles ahead.

Flight 007 was already about one hundred nautical miles to the right or north west of its flight-planned route, R20.

As the 747 approached imaginary waypoint Nabie one hour and thirty minutes into the flight, the co-pilot again watched for the amber alert light to go on, signifying two minutes to arrival at the waypoint. He prepared to make his position report to Anchorage by VHF (very high frequency) radio, giving Anchorage his location, altitude, fuel-on-board check, and estimated time to the next waypoint, Neeva, some 593 nautical miles further along route R20. Two minutes after the alert light came on, the INS display showed the crossing of the correct longitude. The co-pilot, Sohn, transmitted a call to Anchorage Center, but could get no response.

The record shows that at 14:33:47 p.m. GMT, Anchorage Center received an "unintelligible" reply from an "unknown source" to attempts that it had made to contact Flight 007. Again at 14:33:52 the center called "Korean Air 007. Anchorage Center. How do you read?"

The best interpretation the agency could make of a message received at 14:34:18 from what they thought was Flight 007 was, "Ah! It was cut out. Would you try to call once more again."

Finally, at 14:35:11, Korean Air Lines Flight 015, the 747 (with Helms and the other congressmen on board) that had left Anchorage some twenty minutes after Flight 007 and was following it on R20, called Anchorage Center to relay a message for Flight 007 that it had passed over Nabie and would be over Neeva in about one hour fourteen minutes. Flight 015 also passed a fuel report for Flight 007.

Captain Chun finally decided that he was too far out of VHF range to reach Anchorage. He knew his VHF radios were not defective because Sohn could talk with Flight 015.

What Chun decided to do was use his high frequency (HF) radio with its much greater range than a VHF system (which cannot give coverage beyond about 150 nautical miles). On the R20 route, VHF can normally be used as far out as Neeva, some 1,200 miles from Anchorage, because remotely controlled relay stations have been installed within range on islands down the Aleutian chain as far as Shemya. But Flight 007 was not on R20 and had in fact flown well out of the range of the remote VHF stations.

At 14:44:20 GMT Flight 007 contacted the FAA (U.S. Federal Aviation Administration) Flight Service Station at Anchorage on HF radio, giving its position in relation to Nabie and estimating its arrival time at Neeva. The Flight Service Station was requested to pass on the position report to the Anchorage air traffic control center.

KAL Flight 015 passed another message from Flight 007

to the Anchorage air traffic control center at 16:00:46 p.m.
GMT. It advised that Flight 007 was giving its position at
Neeva at 15:58 and was going on to Nippi. The Anchorage
transmission in reply was: "Korean Air 015 understand this
is a position report for Korean Air 007 and advise Korean
Air 007 to ah report Nippi to en-route radio. Thank you
very much."

At 16:00:46, when Flight 007 reported that it was by
waypoint Neeva, its approximate position was some 150
miles north of that imaginary waypoint and therefore that
much off course. It was still over international waters, with
the closest point of the Kamchatka Peninsula about 90
degrees to its right, some 110 nautical miles distant, while the
landfall that it would make on the Kamchatka Peninsula was
some 400 nautical miles ahead.

In the cockpit of Flight 007, still flying in darkness, the
pilots could hear the crackle of voices from other aircraft
reporting their positions. All the voices were male and all
spoke English. The waypoint report at Neeva had been
successfully passed. It would be another hour before the crew
would have to report passing waypoint Nippi, 561 miles
away. When they chose to glance up and out the windscreen
at the vast black nothingness ahead, their eyes could detect
the rapid oscillating glow from the red warning beacons of the
fuselage well behind them. And there was the moon in the
southeast, just a little less than half of it glowing. If the weather radar had been turned on and in the mapping mode,
Captain Chun would have been able to see, at the top left of
the screen by his left knee, two islands coming up at a range of
about 180 miles and, at the right of the screen, the Kamchatka
coast. The radar screen by the co-pilot's right knee, had it
been in the same mode, would have shown the same thing.
Similarly, as the aircraft approached the Kamchatka
landfall, the coastline dead ahead would have been clearly
visible on the radar.

On the other hand, at about the time that the Neeva
waypoint report was made at 16:00:46 GMT, if the pilots had
had their radar switched on and in the weather mode,

whereby the radar searched straight ahead for thunderstorms and weather sufficiently heavy to be picked up by the radar, they might have seen on their screens the blip of a large aircraft passing northbound in front of Flight 007 at a range of about seventy-five miles, although the possibility of their having seen it at that range is highly remote. The aircraft would have been about at Flight 007's level – now 33,000 feet, after 007 had received permission to climb from Anchorage at 16:06:44. Had Flight 007's crew seen it they would have been able to watch this aircraft continue to move north as it crossed their screens to the right. But before it disappeared it would have begun to turn toward the east as if in an orbit.

Both the militarily experienced 747 pilots, who had flown this route many times before, would have guessed, if not known, that the big aircraft their radar was painting was a U.S. Air Force RC-135, another Boeing-made aircraft the Americans used for electronic intelligence.

There are several of these based on the island of Shemya at the southern tip of the Aleutian chain. Shemya is about four hundred miles from the Kamchatka coast and just over one hundred miles southeast of the imaginary waypoint Neeva which Flight 007 said it had just passed, even though it was two hundred miles off course to the north. The Americans operate the RC-135's off the Kamchatka Peninsula as many as twenty days a month and often on the basis of having an aircraft on station twenty-four hours a day, ostensibly to monitor by technical means Soviet compliance with SALT treaties. In reality the RC-135's are supposed to obtain as much intelligence as possible about all Soviet military and naval operations in the area and in particular about the Soviets' long-range missile testing.

The RC-135 was adapted from the Boeing 707 over twenty years ago. It is a much smaller aircraft than the 747, with a wingspan of only 131 feet against the 747's 196 feet, and a length of 136 feet against the 747's 232 feet.

The blue signal light indicating that the KAL 747 was being tracked by radar was glowing steadily. The Soviet military radar net had started to track Flight 007 at about the time that it passed waypoint Nabie, at 14:32 GMT, and was already well off course by a hundred miles and heading for the southern part of the Kamchatka Peninsula.

As the 747 approached the coastline of Kamchatka and the port of Petropavlovsk, six MiG-23 all-weather fighters were ordered aloft from a nearby military airbase, clawing their way upwards into the night to intercept the intruder cruising serenely along at 33,000 feet.

Even though the fighters were directed by radar from the ground and were equipped with their own radar systems, they would not find the 747. Whether Captain Chun had on his navigation lights and his red warning beacons over Kamchatka is not known. They were certainly fully illuminated over Sakhalin.

At 17:09 GMT, when Flight 007 reported to Japanese air control that it was passing waypoint Nippi just a little more than one hundred miles southwest of the southern tip of the Kamchatka Peninsula, the aircraft was in fact just exiting the west coast of Kamchatka over two hundred miles off course to the north of Nippi. Unbeknownst to Captain Chun and his crew, the Soviet Air Defense Force in the region was making an all-out effort to intercept the aircraft and bring it down. Flying steadily on its course of 240 degrees, the jumbo jet headed out over the Sea of Okhotsk, over international waters en route to another Soviet hot spot, Sakhalin Island.

The foiled MiG-23 pilots, having failed in their mission, returned to their Kamchatka base to face whatever wrath awaited them there.

Approaching Sakhalin Island over the international waters of the Sea of Okhotsk and therefore outside Soviet airspace, and about three hundred miles off its flight-planned track, Flight 007 was scheduled to report to Tokyo by radio at 17:07 GMT that it was at waypoint Nokka, some hundred miles to the southeast of the southern tip of the Kuril Islands and the northeastern tip of the Japanese island of Hokkaido.

There had been two previously recorded communications with Japanese air traffic control: the first was at 18:20 GMT when Flight 007 received permission to climb to 35,000 feet, the second when Flight 007 acknowledged, saying that it was leaving altitude 33,000 feet.

The aircraft was just over five hours into its flight. It was still in darkness over the sea of Okhotsk and Sakhalin Island. Most of the 240 passengers were still asleep, their bodies skewed. The cabin lights were still out and the blinds drawn. According to the December 1983 report of the investigating team of the International Civil Aviation Organization (ICAO), the United Nations affiliate, of which the Soviet Union is a member, this is a common practice with carriers flying this route. With little more than two hours left in the flight, the first light of the sun rising in the east would soon appear, chasing the 747 as it moved steadily westward to Seoul. With the first light, the flight attendants would be lifting the blinds, turning on the cabin lights and offering the passengers a delicious breakfast.

But the people of Flight 007 would never have that breakfast. They would never see that dawn.

THE FRUSTRATED Soviet air commander of the Biya region had watched the intruder fly over Petropavlovsk and across the Kamchatka Peninsula without being intercepted by the six MiG-23 aircraft he had sent aloft. The general was furious. He was also afraid he would be sacked. The performance of his combined fighter forces and radar control was dreadful. If his fighters on Sakhalin couldn't intercept and deal with the aircraft that was traversing their sensitive airspace at will, he personally would have to answer to Moscow. The radar people had identified the aircraft first as an RC-135.

Then they had decided it couldn't be an RC-135. This aircraft was travelling far too fast. The RC-135, as the Soviet Air Defense Forces (ADF) radar people well knew – they had tracked them countless times – was an aircraft with antennas and electronic gear that substantially reduced its speed from the normal Boeing 707 of which the RC-135 was a modification.

Furthermore, when the RC-135's arrived off Kamchatka

they would throttle back and reduce speed in order to conserve fuel and stay on station as long as possible.

What the Soviet radar operators understood from experience was that the RC-135's cruised at about 125 knots slower than the Boeing 747's that they had tracked day after day flying down route R20.

The big aircraft they were tracking was flying at a 747's cruising speed. Obviously it was not an RC-135. What was it? Perhaps a 747 loaded with electronic spy gear. Perhaps a bomber. Perhaps a civilian airliner off course. Whatever it was, the aircraft was an intruder over highly sensitive Soviet territory. And it was unidentified.

Every unidentified aircraft that approached within sixty miles of Soviet airspace was immediately reported to the National Command Post of the Air Defense Forces at Kalinin near Moscow. Its course, altitude and speed were displayed so long as the intruder was within the sixty-mile line. A general officer was always on duty in the operations room of the National Command Post for the purpose of giving orders to the appropriate district commanders and to inform his Commander-in-Chief, Marshal Koldunov, of any emergent crisis of the kind that Flight 007 was to present for more than two hours.

The regional commander at Biya had no choice. The intruder could not be allowed to escape. It had to be intercepted. If it did not obey the signals of the interceptor to follow it, then the intruder would have to be shot down. Failure would bring gross embarrassment to the Air Defense Forces. The Politburo would demand answers, as it had done in 1978 when the Korean 707 was finally brought down. If the ADF could not cope with a civilian airliner how could it possibly handle military aircraft on an attack mission? Heads would roll.

The Biya regional general passed his instructions to the commander of the Dolinsk-Sokol air base on Sakhalin Island. He was to commit four of his most experienced pilots. They should be airborne at the best time to maximize their fuel and the opportunity to climb to height and make the intercept before the aircraft exited Soviet airspace. Orders would be given to the pilots through control station Deputat once the interception contact was made. Those orders were issued about 17:00 hours GMT, providing ample time for a thorough briefing of the four selected pilots before the intruder aircraft entered Soviet airspace again. Entry this time would be over Sakhalin Island, if the aircraft continued on its course of 240 degrees.

The orders from Moscow and Biya were being carried out.

The time was 18:03, GMT. The Su-15 all-weather fighter thundered through the frigid air over Sakhalin Island sheathed in the black night, invisible except for the light of a half-moon in the southeast sky that glinted off the aircraft. The single-cannon and twin-rocket-equipped Su-15 was stalking its prey, a big bird intruding into the sovereign airspace of the Soviet Motherland.

Strapped tightly in the ejection seat of the lethal fighter, the pilot focused his eyes on the small radar screen in front of him. He anxiously watched its luminous green face for the first sign of a small dot anywhere on the screen. That blip would tell him he had found his target. The ground radar controllers told him it was fifty kilometers ahead at the altitude at which he had levelled off, 33,000 feet. He was told that the target was maintaining 530 knots per hour on a course of 240 degrees.

The brain of the highly experienced forty-year-old fighter pilot was concentrating not only on what was being fed into it from the radar screen, but also on the information and orders going into it from the radio earphones in the crash helmet clamped on his head.

The words of the ground controller were clear and ungarbled as they were radioed up to the pilot from control station Deputat. The station was on Sakhalin Island near the Dolinsk-Sokol air base from which he had lifted off his Su-15 fighter like a rocket twenty-one minutes earlier. As it had jumped off the runway, the flame from the afterburners of the twin jet engines had bathed the light mist covering the airfield with a fiery orange glare. Then it was gone. With his plane curving upwards almost vertically, the senior pilot steered the vectors that had been given him on the ground by the airfield controller who had handed him off to his operational controller Deputat immediately the Su-15 was airborne.

In less than one minute after he had blasted off from his base, the tremendous thrust from his two Lyulka engines had carried him to the six-mile height at which the intruder target was flying. As he climbed to the designated altitude, the controller had him steer northeast so that he would be positioned to the east of the target, then turn left to come around behind it on its southwesterly course.

In order to conserve fuel, knowing that the target would be cruising at about 530 knots, the Su-15 pilot selected a speed of mach 1.3 or approximately one thousand miles an hour. That would provide him with a more-than-sufficient catch-up speed, which he could rapidly peel off once he established contact with what he was so anxiously looking for and that should show up on his radar at any second.

In his pressurized cocoon of a cockpit, heated to a comfortable 68 degrees Fahrenheit against the killing outside temperature of -50 degrees, the pilot was perspiring profusely in his tight-fitting anti-gravity suit and flying clothing. Even for this highly experienced airman, the blasting takeoff and thrust into the hostile darkness was an enormous physical and intellectual strain, notwithstanding that he had done it hundreds of times. It was like that for most fighter pilots who had to operate in all manner of dreadful weather, night and day. The sudden launch into a foreign, black environment, encapsulated in a state-of-the-art all-weather fighter in which he and his body and brain were required to function at their absolute peak of precision and dexterity, required the maximum of physical and intellectual co-ordination and concentration. The realization that the penalty for failure to execute every step of the flying procedure perfectly might mean death caused the brain to trigger into the bloodstream a super-stimulating flow of the human self-preservation chemical, adrenaline. Its involuntary infusion was followed by a rapid acceleration of the heartbeat as that organ was ordered by the chemical to instantly increase its beat rate in order to get massive amounts of blood to the brain and to the muscles. The generation of perspiration from head to toe immediately followed. Still in the post-takeoff mode and under pressure of the responsibility of finding the target, the pilot was soaking wet inside his flying gear and clothing and his heart was pumping at 145 beats to the minute. While this was a high rate even for a forty year old, it was something that his body could cope with. At that age he was a bit flabby of face and physique but his cardiovascular system, assisted by regular exercise and over twenty years of an average daily vodka consumption at eight to ten ounces, was still in reasonably good shape. Of course, at the parties that the pilots frequently had, his consumption of vodka was much more than that.

But on this night his system was clean. It contained no alcohol, for he had known he had to be on duty starting at dusk the evening before. As a senior member of his squadron, the pilot was in a position of leadership. This meant that he had to set an example, particularly with alcohol, a plague that infested not only the Soviet civilian population and the army and navy but also – and perhaps to an even greater extent – the all-weather fighter pilots stationed in the remote and hostile Sakhalin Island and Kamchatka Peninsula. On their shoulders rested the responsibility for defending Mother Russia from the intrusion of the persistent American RC-135 spy planes that skulked day and night along the edges of Soviet airspace. From their high-altitude vantage points of 30,000 feet or more, they spied hundreds of miles into Soviet territory, listening with their HF (high frequency), VHF (very high frequency), UHF (ultra high frequency), and microwave receivers, and watching, with their exquisite downward-looking radar equipment, all manner of Soviet military operations within the range of the RC-135's elaborate gear.

His head encased in his plastic crash helmet inside the pressurized cockpit of the Su-15, the pilot noticed the perspiration as a drop fell from his left eyebrow. He was momentarily alarmed because, by this time in his flight, the perspiration was usually out of the way as he settled into tracking his target and listening to the instructions from the ground. That was usually the case because these launchings into the night were normally for practice purposes only. They were training missions, so it was easy to settle down after one was straight and level at the assigned altitude.

But tonight was different. He was after an actual intruder into Soviet airspace heading from Alaska on an unmistakable track across the motherland's major bases on the Kamchatka Peninsula and Sakhalin. Whatever the aircraft was, it was on a spying mission. Whatever it was, it was a target. It had to be intercepted and stopped. It was not his responsibility to identify it. It didn't matter to him what it was. His duty was to find it and try to signal it to follow him. If he couldn't do that, he would have to take his orders from the ground as to what to do. But, again, it was not his responsibility to identify the aircraft. The identification matter had already been sorted out by the authorities on the ground. He knew that the orders given to him in the air would come from the regional commander from some general or marshal above him. Whatever the order, he would obey it.

But he did wonder what the target was. It was probably some type of U.S. spy plane intentionally crossing Soviet airspace to soak up by photographic and electronic means whatever information it could about what was going on in the hypersensitive military, naval and rocket installations in the area.

Or perhaps it was a civilian airliner loaded with electronic gear in the same way that some Aeroflot aircraft were, claiming that it was accidentally off-course when in fact it was capturing secret Soviet signals and transmitting them back to (perhaps) an RC-135 prowling in the sky to the east, outside of Soviet airspace. If it was one of those Korean 747's doing just that, the Soviet pilot could see in his mind's eye the oriental face of the Korean captain, whoever he was, contentedly sitting in the cockpit of his 747, heading happily across Sakhalin Island for Seoul, believing that he could overfly Soviet territory in the middle of a dark night and nothing would happen.

Whatever the aircraft was, it had entered Soviet airspace about an hour before the Su-15 pilot had been called in by the duty operations officer and briefed on the interception mission ordered by Moscow through the Biya region commander.

During the briefing the pilot had been given all the information on the aircraft that was available: height, course and airspeed – but no identification. The intruder was on an electronic spying mission and had to be stopped. Its subsonic flying speed indicated that it could be a bomber, a reconnaissance aircraft or a commercial passenger aircraft equipped for electronic espionage. Its point of origin was probably Anchorage, Alaska. It had overflown Petropavlovsk. It would overfly the naval base on Sakhalin Island unless it was stopped. Its ultimate destination was unknown.

The orders for the pilot of the Su-15 and the pilots of the three MiG-23's that were also being sent up for the same mission were to find and intercept the damn thing! The Kamchatka fighers had failed, to the high embarrassment of the Biya general and the ADF commander-in-chief in Moscow. The orders from Moscow were that the intruder must be found and dealt with. This sort of deliberate intrusion had been happening far too often in the Biya region. So it was up to the four pilots from the Dolinsk-Sokol air regiments to do the interception. They must not fail. As a matter of honor and duty to the motherland they must not fail!

When one of them made the interception, he would be given instructions through Deputat what actions to carry out.

What about identification? "Identification is not your responsibility. The target has been identified as a hostile intruder carrying out an espionage mission against the Motherland. You may be able to see the target, you may not. The fact is, there have been electronic emissions from the target which indicate clearly that it is a spy plane. So whatever the aircraft is, there are grounds for shooting it down if it fails to respond to signals."

To shoot or not to shoot was a decision the pilot would not have to make. His function was to put his rocket platform, his aircraft, into a position behind the target so that those rockets could be launched to destroy the intruder when the order to do so was given by headquarters and transmitted to the pilot by the ground controller, Deputat.

So it was that at 18:03 GMT in the early morning hours of September 1, 1983, the Su-15 pilot was in his all-weather fighter at 33,000 feet over Sakhalin Island waiting for the target aircraft to appear on his radar screen. His orders were to transmit in the clear. It was not necessary to attempt to use a code, even though the Japanese would be monitoring his transmissions. The pilot knew that the Deputat VHF transmissions made to him from the ground on Sakhalin were beyond the range of Japanese VHF reception, and so would not be monitored by Japanese ground stations. On the other hand they might be heard by a prowling but distant American RC-135 and certainly by the aircraft he was chasing, if indeed it was an American Air Force spy plane.

At 18:05:53 he reported to Deputat, "805. On course 240," which meant that he was on the same course that the target was on. He was behind it and, if the Deputat instructions were right, he was following it and closing up the distance.

Three seconds later he shouted into his microphone, "805. I see it!"

From that moment until 18:26:27, when he reported he was breaking off the attack, there was a staccato of replies and reports as the Su-15 pilot responded to the directions and orders from Deputat.

18:06:00   "805. Roger. Understood. I'm flying behind."

18:08:06   "805. On course 260. . . . Understood."

This meant that he was behind the 747, then turned his aircraft slightly to the right as he caught up with the larger plane.

18:09   "805. Yes, it has turned. . . . The target is 80 degrees to my left."

This meant that his aircraft was off to the right of the target and was almost even with or abreast of it. In order to make this report he would have to see the 747 clearly. It would not be on his radar scope.

18:09:44   "805. Course 240. . . . Roger."

18:10:35   "805. Course 220."

The Su-15 had turned left from its position parallel to the target on course 240 degrees (the course of the 747), through to 220 degrees, which would bring the Soviet fighter up on the left side of the jumbo jet, toward the proper position for signalling to the intercepted aircraft's captain in accordance with ICAO rules.

18:11:20   "805. 8,000 meters (26,247 feet). . . . Roger."

When he executed that order he would drop below the target, which was flying at 33,000 feet.

18:12:10   "805. I see it visually and on radar."

This is the third statement confirming that he could clearly see the target. With this pilot's background and experience, there can be no question that in seeing the aircraft, with its distinctive hump at the top front of the fuselage where the cockpit was located, he could identify it for what it was – a Boeing 747. The moonlight was at 45 per cent and the moon 60 degrees above the horizon and in the southeast. From his position to the left or right of the 747 he would be able to see the civilian markings on the white aircraft by the light of the moon. If the fin logo lights of the 747 were on, its identity would have been doubly clear.

18:13:26   "805. The target isn't responding to I.F.F."

I.F.F., which stands for "Identification: Friend or Foe," is a means of identifying friendly or hostile aircraft. In approved procedures, the intercepting fighter directs the unidentified target to switch to a predetermined radio frequency for further communications. Only friendly aircraft know which radio frequency to tune in; an aircraft which is challenged and fails to respond is therefore identified as a foe.

However, only military aircraft use the I.F.F. system; and only they are equipped with it.

This challenge by the Soviet fighter pilot could be evidence that he thought the aircraft was military. On the other hand, his I.F.F. challenge might have been part of the drill or routine he was trained to carry out whether or not the aircraft he had intercepted had civilian rather than military markings. After all, the 747 might be military but painted with civilian markings as a disguise.

18:13:35 "805. The target's course is 240 degrees."

This report confirmed that the 747 was still flying on the course it was on when he intercepted it, notwithstanding the report at 18:09, "Yes, it has turned." In fact at 18:15:08 the Su-15 pilot stated, "The target's course is still the same . . . 240."

18:18:03 "805. I see it!" (Emphatic)

There is no question he saw it and saw it well. The fact that he did not report what the aircraft was confirms that it was not his duty or responsibility to identify the aircraft or to report any identification to the ground. The fact that he saw a 747 with civilian markings on it was of no concern to him. The people on the ground had the responsibility for identification and for all decisions as to how to deal with the target intruder.

18:18:34 "805. The A.N.O. (Air Navigational Lights) are burning. The (strobe) light is flashing."

The ICAO report stated that, contrary to the tapes, the KAL 747 was not equipped with strobe lights. Instead it had red rotating warning beacons on the fuselage.

18:19:02 "805. I am closing on the target."

This transmission means that he is coming up behind the 747.

18:19:08 "805. They do not see me."

This statement could be in response to a question from Deputat about whether there were any signs that the 747 crew had seen him.

18:20:08 "805. Fiddlesticks. I'm going. That is, my Z.G. (indicator) is lit."

His reference to the Z.G. indicator means that the radar-guided missile warhead is locked on to the target. He is ready to fire if the order is given. But he is getting more instructions from Deputat in rapid order. At 18:20:12 he says, "Answering," five seconds later, "I answered." Then, in order to carry out the instruction he receives in the next five seconds, he says, "Need to approach it," meaning that to carry out the order he would have to get closer to the target.

18:20:30 "805. I am turning lock-on off and I'm approaching the target."

His orders just received had been to turn the lock-on of the missiles off. This he has done. The order is now to use his cannon. To do so he has to get closer to the target. In order for the shells to be effective – either as a warning (if some of them were tracer shells which burn brilliantly as they travel through the air and are therefore easily seen) or if the shells were to be used to attempt to shoot the 747 down – the pilot would want to be as close as he could behind the 747, yet clear of the powerful turbulence caused by its wake. Having regard also for the relatively short range of the cannon, he should have been sitting about 1,500 feet behind the target because the maximum range of the Su-15 cannon is one kilometer or less than one mile. But at this point the Su-15 was about six kilometers behind.

18:20:49 "805. I am firing cannon bursts."

He fired 120 rounds in four bursts. If they were aimed at the aircraft and hit it, there is no evidence from the pilots of Flight 007 that they were aware their aircraft had been hit. Similarly if the rounds were tracer shells designed to get the 747's attention, the crew did not seen them. These conclusions follow from the fact that, at 18:20, when the Su-15 pilot was firing his cannon, Flight 007 was calling Japanese air traffic control to ask permission to climb to 35,000 feet.

Japanese ATC gave permission and Flight 007 responded by saying that it was leaving altitude 33,000 feet for the higher altitude. There was no report of anything unusual, let alone cannon fire or tracer shells.

With the permission to climb given, Captain Chun turned the altitude setting up to 35,000 feet. The aircraft automatically responded. The nose lifted slightly as it began the short climb of 2,000 feet. The captain may have increased the engine power for the climb or he may not. Either way, the speed of the airplane decreased during the climb phase.

18:21:35 "805. The target's light is blinking. I have approached the target to a distance of about two kilometers (1.2 miles)."

18:22:02 "805. The target is decreasing speed."

The Su-15 pilot believed that the decrease in speed was an evasion tactic by the 747. However, the aircraft was simply climbing to the height approved by Japanese air traffic control.

18:22:17 "805. I am going around it. I'm already moving in front of the target."

As the speed of the 747 decreased, the Su-15 pilot couldn't slow down fast enough to stay behind it, so he found himself in front of the jumbo jet.

His chatter with Deputat is constant as the orders and questions are fired at him from the ground.

18:22:23 "805. I have increased speed."

18:22:29 "805. No. It is decreasing speed."

18:22:42 "805. It should have been earlier. How can I chase it? I am already abeam of the target."

18:22:55 "805. Now I have to fall back a bit from the target."

18:23:05 "805. Repeat."

18:23:10 "805. The target's altitude is 33,000 feet."

18:23:18 "805. For me it is located 70 degrees to the left."

He is still almost abeam of or parallel to the 747 and off to its right.

18:23:37 "805. I am dropping back. Now I will try rockets."

This statement implies that he will try rockets instead of the cannon and that his earlier use of the cannon was not for signalling but was an attempt to shoot the 747 down as ordered through Deputat. Almost one minute later he acknowledges an instruction from Deputat and confirms that his rockets are locked on to the target.

18:24:22 "805. Roger. I am in lock-on."

18:25:11 "805. I am closing on the target. Am in lock-on. Distance to target is eight kilometers (five miles)."

18:25:46 "805. Z.G."

Again these are the code letters that mean his missile radar warhead is locked on to the target and he is ready to fire.

The KAL 747 and all the people in it were doomed. It took two seconds for the lethal rockets to reach the huge aircraft, detonate and instantly kill every soul on board except the flight-deck crew, who survived long enough to transmit, at 18:27 GMT sharp (the Su-15 pilot had reported thirty-eight seconds earlier that the target was destroyed) a garbled communication that sounded to experts like "Radio . . . Korean Air 007 . . . All engines . . . Rapid decompression . . . 101 . . . 00" (which might have meant the word "Two") and, finally, "Delta."

That transmission lasted only eighteen seconds.

The total time from the Su-15 pilot's report of destruction to the end of the last transmission from co-pilot Sohn in the 747 was less than one minute. As the transmission died so did the crew, locked in their flight deck.

3

DID THEY KNOW
THEY WERE THERE?

WHEN THE Korean Air Lines 747, Flight 007 (KE007), was
shot down, it had been in Soviet airspace for over two hours,
except for the time it took to fly across international waters
over the Sea of Okhotsk. At the point of its destruction over
Sakhalin Island it was approximately 311 miles north of its
flight-planned route along R20.

Nevertheless the crew of Flight 007 had reported passing
the required waypoints at Nabie, Neeva and Nippi off the
southern tip of the Kamchatka Peninsula just as if the aircraft
were truly over those waypoints. The Nabie passage had to
be reported via KAL Flight 015 at 14:35 GMT. The next
communication was direct from Flight 007 by high-frequency
radio to the Flight Service Station at Anchorage at 14:44:20,
confirming the Nabie passage. Flight 007 reported its
position at Neeva using VHF through Flight 015 at 16:00:46
and estimated it would be at Nippi at 17:08.

At 17:09, almost exactly at the time predicted, Flight 007
made its first radio (high frequency) contact with Tokyo air
traffic control (Narita), reported its position "over Nippi
17:07" and estimated it would be at Nokka waypoint off the
southern end of the Kuril Islands at 18:26.

The aircraft was not over Nippi. It was just crossing the
westerly shore of the Kamchatka Peninsula, was about to
cross the Sea of Okhotsk and was some 250 NM to the
northwest of Nippi and its flight-planned route.

At 18:20 GMT, some six minutes before it was destroyed,
Flight 007 received permission from Japanese air traffic con-

trol to climb to 35,000 feet. At that time the aircraft was over Sakhalin Island. This was one of the first direct communications with air traffic control from the time Flight 007 had been cleared en route by Anchorage.

There was nothing wrong with Flight 007's VHF radios, and the captain and co-pilot knew it. If there had been something wrong, Sohn would not have been able to transmit to Flight 015, flying approximately twenty minutes behind him in time, and actually on route R20. Sohn's inability to reach Anchorage air traffic control on VHF ought to have been strong evidence for an experienced pilot like Captain Chun that he was out of radio range when he should not have been.

The basic question is this: Did Captain Chun and his co-pilot know where they actually were, miles off R20 instead of where they reported themselves to be, when they passed the Nabie, Neeva and Nippi checkpoints; or had they inadvertently strayed off course, believing that they were actually following route R20?

If they deliberately selected a course on or near the Great Circle Route out of Anchorage direct to Seoul, then a second question follows. It is, simply, Why? That is a quite different matter, which will be dealt with only if the answer to the main question is: Yes, they knew where they were.

If the aircraft's black boxes had been retrieved, the answer to the main question might have been found. On the other hand, it might not, depending upon the boxes' condition after taking the full force of the explosion from one of the Su-15's rockets. Both of the black boxes carried by the Boeing 747 were installed at the rear near the airliner's tail, above the coat rack in front of the rear left lavatories where normally they are considered to be virtually indestructible.

One of the machines was for recording in-flight data such as airspeed, altitude and direction. The second box, a cockpit voice recorder, was to tape the last thirty minutes of conversation, the sound of warning horns and other noises in the aircraft's cockpit. The black boxes are actually painted orange, a colour easy to spot in wreckage.

Small batteries in an attached underwater acoustic beacon

give enough power to send out electronic beeps for thirty days. With the proper equipment, these can be heard under water. This was the signal that the Soviet, American and Japanese ships were listening for, and which the Americans actually heard as they searched for Flight 007's black boxes in 300 to 2,500 feet of water just to the west of Moneron Island in the Sea of Japan.

The black boxes are water-proofed and encased in steel. They are about the size of a breadbox – 9" × 5" × 15". They are designed to survive a 5,000-pound crush test and a 2,000-degree fire for thirty minutes. In considering whether the black boxes would survive the tremendous explosion that occurred when one of the Su-15's ANAB rockets detonated in the tail, it is important to note that the boxes were built to withstand an impact more than one thousand times the force of gravity. The sections of the KAL 747's tail that were found clearly demonstrate that it was ripped into many pieces by the force of the ANAB's blast. It follows that the black boxes could have received an explosion force close to or beyond their strength limits.

Even if the cockpit voice recorder (CVR) black box had been found, it might not have provided all of the information the searchers were looking for. There are two reasons for this.

The first is that the CVR, as already stated, records only the last thirty minutes of the conversation and noises in the cockpit. On this flight, that would have meant that the crew's voices could first be heard only when the aircraft was over the Sea of Okhotsk, having left Soviet airspace over the Kamchatka Peninsula. At that late stage of the flight there would be little prospect of the crew's talking about having strayed off-course either inadvertently or intentionally.

The box might, however, have supplied information about whether the 747's crew had seen the Soviet fighter approaching on the right, then on the left, or at all; about whether the crew had seen the tracers that were allegedly fired; or, indeed, about whether the aircraft had been struck by cannon shells.

The second reason that the black boxes might not have

provided information is this: even if the CVR had survived, difficulties with transcribing the voices and sounds recorded on the CVR tape are common, especially when the crew members are not using the radio transmitter or the aircraft's interphone. Inasmuch as the recording is being done by an area microphone which is supposed to absorb the total aural environment, it is sometimes most difficult to differentiate between speech and other sounds.

Notwithstanding these shortcomings of the CVR black box, it was mandatory that every effort be made by both sides to retrieve both boxes, especially the cockpit voice recorder.

The boxes were not found. The water-activated batteries of the "pingers" became exhausted, and by the middle of November the search in the deep waters was abandoned.

So without the black boxes and the information on their tapes, the question whether the captain of Flight 007 was there intentionally or accidentally can only be answered by examining all the known facts and arriving at a judgment.

A staggering number of theories have been presented in all media, but especially in the press, about how Flight 007 got over three hundred miles off its flight-planned route R20. These hypotheses range from a simple navigational error – such as the transposition of the figures being fed into the three interlocked Inertial Navigation Systems – to the proposition that the captain knew exactly where he was and was there intentionally.

To arrive at a conclusion on the question of inadvertence or intentionality requires an examination first of the two key navigation tools that the KAL 747's flight crew had available to them and second of how they could have used or misused those tools.

The primary tools are the Inertial Navigation Systems (three on board) and the 747's weather radar (two on board), which can be used as a secondary source of information to confirm the primary navigation information of the INS.

The KAL 747, Flight 007, carried three INS devices to provide primary navigaton. All three were Litton Industries LTN-72R INS units. INS systems were initially developed to enable ballistic missiles to travel on a preset course to enemy targets many thousands of miles distant. The systems are totally self-contained and need no direction from radio or other signals.

When they are in operation the systems continuously sense every movement of the aircraft about all three axis. They constantly calculate where these movements are taking the plane, from its initial position standing at the gate (which is programmed into the computer) to the precise position, a hundred, a thousand or five thousand miles away, to which the pilot wishes the aircraft to go.

In order to provide a cross-check and back-up for each other, and for reliability and safety, there were three INS systems on board the Boeing 747. Each was completely independent of the other, but all three could be tied together as one if the captain so chose. In the photograph of the 747 cockpit (see photo section) the three INS keyboards are circled. It can be seen that they are readily visible to both pilots. The digital numbers and figures glowing on their keyboard faces would stand out in a darkened cockpit. The INS keyboard (Figure 2:1, p. 20) enables crew members to insert into the INS computers the latitudes and longitudes of the point of departure and of the waypoints. Each flight route is assigned a name (such as R20). The waypoints marked on the en-route map at specific pre-designated latitudinal and longitudinal positions are in fact imaginary. They are given names such as Nabie, Neeva, Nippi and the like.

The INS units may be separately programmed; or all three can be programmed at the same time in the "remote" mode from the keyboard of one unit. The choice is up to the captain. Some prefer to program each unit separately in order to provide a programming check that ensures that the latitudes and longitudes being punched in are in fact going in correctly. In this event the third machine is programmed as a working spare. If the "remote" approach is taken, exactly the same waypoint and destination co-ordinates that are punched into one machine are automatically inserted into the other two.

The INS can receive and act upon a maximum of nine programmable points: the point of departure and nine en-route waypoints. When coupled with the autopilot system, sometimes known as "George", the INS directs the aircraft – that is, navigates it – from the takeoff point to each of the waypoints and, finally, to the destination, when it is inserted.

To assist the crew, an amber alert light on the INS keyboard face will automatically come on two minutes before a waypoint is reached. When the aircraft is at a waypoint, the amber light will glow for two minutes.

It must be understood, however, that the waypoint alert light is the result of the INS calculating distance. That is, the waypoint alert light will come on when the aircraft has flown the *distance* the INS has been told it will fly between any two waypoints. However, the automatic pilot, "George" (its five position switch and surrounding panel are shown in Figure 3:1), may be in the HDG (heading) mode rather than the INS mode. This means that the aircraft flies according to its last "heading" (the course the aircraft was on when the heading position on the switch was selected), and may in reality be some considerable distance to the right or left of a particular waypoint. Even if this is the case, and the aircraft is not actually at the waypoint, the amber alert light will still come on to tell the pilot that the distance to that waypoint has been covered. Meanwhile, the aircraft could be two hundred miles or more from the waypoint. And, in fact, Flight 007 was more than two hundred miles to the northwest abeam waypoint Nippi when the Nippi waypoint warning light came on. Among other things, that told the captain and co-pilot that they should report to Anchorage air traffic control, as was mandatory, and that they were at Nippi, when in reality they were over two hundred miles northwest of it. Did they know they were there? (See the Chapter 2 map.)

The human errors or faulty procedures that might have taken Flight 007 from Anchorage to Sakhalin Island are as follows:

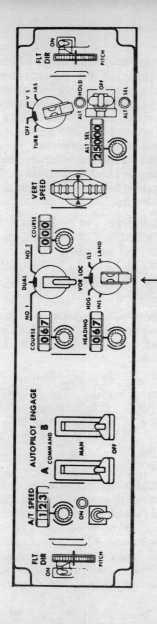

NAVIGATION MODE SWITCH

Figure 3:1 Autopilot Flight Director Mode Selector Panel. (For the location of this panel, see the picture of the Boeing 747 cockpit in photo section.)

1. On the run from Anchorage to Bethel, the five-position switch that sets the automatic pilot into various optional modes of operation may have been set on Heading rather than on INS with the crew intending to turn it to INS after Bethel passage. The aircraft's course would therefore be 246 degrees. At Bethel passage (where Flight 007 passed Bethel twelve nautical miles to the north instead of over it), the crew may have failed to select INS with the result that the aircraft simply followed the 246-degree heading it was on. This would have taken it on the track it followed over Kamchatka and Sakhalin to its point of destruction.

2. The numbers and the co-ordinates at Nokka may have been transposed so that the fifth set of co-ordinates (for Nokka) were incorrectly punched into the machine as N47 23.3 E142 28.8, instead of N42 23.3 E147 28.8. The incorrect co-ordinates were those that would have taken the aircraft to the location where it was destroyed.

3. When the waypoints were punched into the Inertial Navigation System's nine waypoint slots, the track from the takeoff point direct to Seoul may have gone in accidentally.

4. The waypoints may have been put correctly into one INS, and only the Seoul co-ordinates into the second – the latter programming enabling the pilots easily to determine fuel/time "howgozit" information. The selection of that INS system might then inadvertently have been coupled with the autopilot rather than with the INS system that had all the correct waypoints plugged into it.

There are other scenarios of pilot error and inadvertence that might explain how Flight 007 crossed the Kamchatka Peninsula and arrived over Sakhalin Island without the crew knowing where they were or, to put it another way, while believing they were following route R20. In particular the Investigation Team of the International Civil Aviation Organization (ICAO) has suggested the first scenario – that the aircraft was on the Heading mode at 246 degrees; or, alternatively, that there was a ten degree error in inserting the present position (ramp) co-ordinates. These suggestions will be discussed in due course. But first let us consider the four possibilities previously listed.

Did the crew forget to switch from the Heading mode to INS as the aircraft passed twelve miles to the north of Bethel, so that the 747 stayed on the Heading mode, steering the 246-degree course that would have taken them to the destruction point? If that is what happened, it means that the two experienced pilots sat in their cockpit for over five hours, with the autopilot selector switch straight ahead of them at eye level and at arm's length, yet failed to see that the selector switch was on Heading instead of INS (see photo of Boeing 747 cockpit). Impossible to believe.

Furthermore, even if the automatic pilot was in the Heading mode, one INS unit would have been selected to distance/time (the unit that should be controlling the autopilot), while the other INS (in this case, one other) should have been selected to cross-track/track error, This is the XTK/TKE point on the INS selector switch at the bottom left-hand corner of the INS control box (see Figure 2:1, p. 20). When selected, the track angle error from 0 to 180 degrees is shown on the right numerical display at the top of the control box. The cross-track distance from 0 to 399.9 nautical miles is shown on the left numerical display. Thus the crew can find out if and how far they are off track and what heading they have to take up to get back on track simply by selecting the XTK/TKE position. When the amber alert light on the INS units came on two minutes before a waypoint, at least one of the units should have been displaying cross-track/track error, which would show *clearly* if the aircraft was off the pre-selected INS routing for R20.

As has already been discussed, the amber waypoint warning lights would dutifully come on as the INS measured the distance flown, even though the 747 was "a considerable distance" abeam and to the west of the correct waypoint location. Furthermore, the course shown on the 747's compasses would probably not alert the crew to a course deviation. The magnetic variation, which changes from +18 degrees east at Bethel through 0 to -9 degrees west at Sakhalin when flying a compass course of 246 degrees, produces a track over the ground of 264 degrees near Bethel and 237 degrees near Sakhalin – if the wind is disregarded. Knowing about these wide variations and relying on their three sophisticated INS units, which were all apparently functioning in accordance with the programming the crew had put into them, the pilots would not have depended on the compasses to tell them that they were off course.

Again it is impossible to believe that the pilots would leave the clearly visible autopilot selector switch in the Heading mode for five hours and, for the same length of time, fail to carry out any cross checks with the other two INS units.

The same line of reasoning applies to the possibility that a direct track to Seoul went into the INS accidentally; and to the possibility that waypoints were entered correctly in one system while the leg direct to Seoul was selected on the second system and the autopilot channel for the direct route was selected inadvertently.

There *is* a recorded case in which the autopilot selector switch was left on the Heading mode for possibly three or four hours. The American National Aeronautics and Space Administration (NASA) receives and compiles reports of cases in which Inertial Navigation Systems have malfunctioned, in which crew members have made errors in programming their computers, and in which they have failed to properly monitor the INS in flight. In one report of an aircraft flying between Japan and Oakland, California, the captain discovered that he was 400 kilometers (250 miles) north of his course. In that case the autopilot was switched to the Heading position instead of to INS, with the result that the aircraft held to its last heading rather than following the INS instructions. A crew member discovered the error by monitoring the second INS. The reporting pilot wrote, "It is not known how the autopilot . . . was switched to the wrong position. Equipment malfunction or inadvertent crew action is suspected." It is important to note that the error was discovered by cross-checking.

It is reasonable to expect that, with two highly experienced pilots at the controls of Flight 007 one of them would have caught the Heading switch selection error long before the aircraft was destroyed. Indeed, it is reasonable to expect that the error would not have occurred in the first place.

As to the possibility that the co-ordinates were transposed while they were being punched into the INS for Nokka, this theory assumes that Flight 007 would have correctly followed the R20 route as far down as Nippi, off the southern tip of the Kamchatka Peninsula, since the co-ordinates of all of the other waypoints were correctly inserted at Anchorage. If this theory were correct, the 747 would not have crossed the Kamchatka Peninsula (which it did) and would not have started off course shortly after it left Anchorage. Furthermore when it went by waypoint Nippi, the autopilot, directed by the INS, would have turned the aircraft to the right by approximately thirty degrees. That turn would not have been expected by the pilots, who would immediately have been alerted that something was wrong. It cannot be argued that they both might have been asleep when that happened, because the co-pilot passed a waypoint report at that time.

One other navigation-assist device was available to the 747 crew. This is the onboard weather radar system. Its function is primarily to enable the pilots to see weather build-ups ahead of them and to be able to select routes through the least turbulent areas (it is mandatory to avoid the center core of thunderstorms because of violent turbulence and hail). The two Bendix weather radar systems installed in the KAL 747 could also be switched to look down and ahead so that they showed the contours of coastlines and other ground features such as mountains. Land could be detected up to two hundred miles ahead when the radar was in this "mapping" mode. The Kamchatka Peninsula and the Kuril Islands are high, prominent and rocky – beautiful radar targets. With

route R20 running so close to the Kurils, the pilot could stay
out of trouble areas by keeping the islands about a hundred
miles to his right while inbound toward Japan and Seoul. The
radar screen is conveniently located for the captain by his left
knee and for the co-pilot by his right knee. The on/off and
mapping-mode selector switch is at the crew's fingertips. If
the pilots had their weather radar on and in the mapping
mode as the 747 approached the Kamchatka Peninsula or
overflew it, they would have known from it exactly where
they were. But if the pilots had it on and knew where they
were, then that could only mean that they had selected that
course deliberately.

Another point. Even if the pilots had switched the radar on
in its mapping mode at the time they were approaching
Sakhalin as a supplementary check to find out where they
were, they might readily confuse Sakhalin's coastline with
Hokkaido's, and think that, although they had made a nor-
therly error in their navigation, it was not as great or
dangerous as the one they had actually made.

We know that the pilots were using and relying on their
Inertial Navigaton Systems. What we do *not* know is whether they were using the weather radars in their mapping
mode.

However, Captain Kim Chang Kyu, the pilot of the
Korean Air Lines Boeing 707 that was shot down by the
Soviets in April 1978 and who, as a 747 captain, now
regularly flies the Anchorage-Seoul route, has said, referring
to approaches to Kamchatka, the Kurils and Japan,
"Everybody uses weather radar in that area."

Kim has also said, with regard to the Inertial Navigation
Systems, that the standard procedure is for another member
of the crew to check the numbers logged in each time. As to
putting latitude numbers into the computer for longitude and
vice-versa (as might have been done for waypoint Nokka),
Kim was of the opinion that, "A mistake like that is very hard
to imagine."

In order to check out the Inertial Navigational System and

the possibilities that I have already discussed, I arranged for a flight from Anchorage to Seoul by route R20 and also by the Great Circle Route over Kamchatka and Sakhalin. The crew who flew me were: Captain Don Stinson, Air Canada's Chief Pilot, B-747; Captain Howard Malone, a highly experienced 747 pilot; and First Officer John Bradshaw, another 747 expert. Before you wonder how we dared fly through the highly sensitive airspace of the paranoid Soviets at the risk of meeting the same fate as Flight 007, let me tell you that we did the flight in Air Canada's 747 simulator located at Toronto's Lester B. Pearson International Airport. All of the waypoints were loaded into the simulator's INS systems and off we went from Anchorage to Bethel and then down R20 to Seoul. The required co-ordinates were inserted into the simulator's two INS systems using the "remote" mode.

The trip to Seoul direct from Anchorage and Bethel was much simpler than R20 because the crew decided that Captain Chun would not have departed R20 until he passed the Neeva waypoint. They so reasoned because, if he was not actually at Neeva when he reported that he was, the American military radar would have known. On the other hand, there has been no public indication that U.S. military radar were tracking or had any information on Flight 007. If they did have any information, they would probably not divulge it for fear of prejudicing the security of their radar installations in the area. In any event, the ICAO Investigation Team's report subsequently gave us the information that Flight 007 passed Bethel twelve NM to the north and so was off course there long before Neeva.

If the 747 had gone off course after Neeva, either intentionally or inadvertently, for any of the reasons previously mentioned, the course from Neeva to the point of destruction over Sakhalin would have required a right turn of some thirty degrees. As previously noted, the crew would have detected an unscheduled turn of that magnitude and immediately corrected the error. Furthermore the track across Kamchatka from Neeva to Sakhalin would have meant crossing the peninsula much farther south of the route that the Soviets claim the 747 followed over Petropavlovsk. The United States has denied the accuracy of the Soviet route claim.

Also against the "right-turn-at-Neeva" theory is the fact that we know VHF radios were serviceable. The crew would have been able to transmit to and receive from Anchorage through the Aleutian relay system if the 747 was in fact at Neeva. Instead it was out of range. At Neeva Flight 007 would have been only 130 miles from the U.S. Air Force base on Shemya Island and the powerful VOR radio navigational station there. The 747 should have been able to get bearing and distance on the Shemya VOR as a check to confirm its position. In reality however, the 747 was well off course to the northwest and already out of the VHF maximum range of about three hundred miles.

Some of the information and conclusions that came out of the flight with Captain Stinson and his colleagues are these:

1. If the Korean captain had deliberately selected the Great Circle Route direct from Anchorage via Bethel to Seoul, he would have saved only 178 nautical miles and roughly 7,000 pounds ($1,000 worth) of fuel. The time saved would have been about twenty minutes. With an operating cost per hour for the 747 of about $8,000, the saving would probably have been about $2,600 (U.S.).

2. The U.S. military have radar with Tacans (Tactical Air Navigation Equipment - UHF Omni Range transmitters which aircraft can use to navigate and to check their positions) at Shemya Island and would have seen the 747 if it had passed Neeva on course (but not if Flight 007 was already well off course, some 340 nautical miles north west of Shemya).

All three pilots were unanimous on this point: when Flight 007 made its Nippi waypoint position report, the co-pilot knew where he was. "He had to know where he was when he made the Nippi report," Stinson said.

Where he was when he made the Nippi report, at 17:09 GMT, was over the western edge of the Kamchatka Peninsula. A few minutes earlier Flight 007 had overflown Petropavlovsk, with six MiG-23's trying to catch it.

That conclusion is compelling and inescapable. The only valid alternative is that the incorrect selection of the Heading mode on the autopilot box remained undetected for over five hours. Given all the cross-checks that were available and the high experience of both pilots, that alternative just does not stand up.

The answer to the question, "Did the 747's crew know the aircraft was off course?" is, "Yes, they knew exactly where they were from the time they left Anchorage through the false waypoint checks that they transmitted past Kamchatka and over Sakhalin Island to their destruction."

The final, crucial question about the route flown by Captain Chun is: "Why was he intentionally there?"

4

THE KAL PILOTS
AND THE COMPANY

IF WE ARE to understand why KAL Flight 007 knowingly took a course that placed it deep inside sensitive Soviet territory, information about the men in the cockpit of the 747 is important. Equally relevant are the history of Korean Air Lines – "where it came from" – and the attitude and policies of the airline and its management.

Captain Chun and co-pilot Sohn have already been introduced. Chun's reputation was that of a highly capable, experienced and aggressive pilot. He was totally dedicated to the objectives of his country and of his airline. He was a "model pilot." In 1982 he had received a citation for his accident-free record. Chun was completely familiar with the North Pacific (NORPAC) route, having flown it from Anchorage for the last five years. In the South Korean Air Force, the organization that produced virtually all of KAL's pilots, he had been a recognized leader, rising to the rank of colonel before he went to Korean Air Lines in 1972.

"Aggressive" is the word that best characterized Captain Chun. It is also the word that best characterizes both Korean Air Lines as a corporation and the two brothers who control and run it, Choong Hoon Cho and Choong Kun Cho. They have a diversified transportation organization known as the Han Jin Group of which Mr. Hoon Cho (known also as Harry Cho) is the chairman. This sixty-three-year-old industrialist has the characteristics of many other South Korean business leaders. He is hard-driving and disciplined, a no-

nonsense man whose forceful notion of corporate management has made Korean Air Lines one of the most aggressive and rapidly growing air services in the world.

In 1969 the Han Jin Group took over from the South Korean government its deficit-ridden national air carrier and the successful struggle to turn the airline around began. Starting as a small trucking operation, Mr. Hoon Cho's transportation group had received a major boost from contracts for hauling drinking water by truck to U.S. troops during the Korean War. The company and the fleet of trucks grew. During the Viet Nam War, the Han Jin organization was an important hauler of supplies for U.S. forces. Under the dynamic leadership of Harry Cho, the company gained the reputation of being able to deliver ammunition to hotspots where other truckers refused to go. Mr. Cho had money incentives from the United States Army to deliver the goods to dangerous locations, and he in turn gave incentives to his drivers to get their trucks there despite the risks. Incentives, bonuses and rewards go to those employees who perform and who save money for the Han Jin Group or for Korean Air Lines. Harry Cho's policies have meant incredible growth.

The revenues of Korean Air Lines when Han Jin took control in 1969 were $6.8 million with about five hundred employees. By 1982, revenues were $1.1 billion, an increase of about 180 times the 1969 mark. There were then about ten thousand workers. When Harry Cho took over KAL it had one jet and seven propeller-driven aircraft and was a domestic carrier only. By December 1982 it had a fleet of forty-one aircraft. Of that fleet, twenty-seven were wide-bodied jetliners of which fourteen were 747's, five were DC10's and eight were A-300's, known as the "European Airbus". Now Korean Air Lines offers at least 130 international flights a week with destinations in the United States, Europe, the Middle East, Southeast Asia, Japan and Africa.

The growth since 1969 has been nothing short of astonishing. However, this incredible growth has also been expensive. The company has incurred huge capital debts to buy its ever-expanding fleet of ultra-costly, sophisticated aircraft. The company's balance sheet, as of December 31, 1982, showed a debt burden of $1.1 billion, the equivalent to its revenues during that year.

During 1980-81, the cumulative losses of KAL were $47.8 million. In 1982 the airline showed a profit of $6 million after chairman Harry Cho initiated a series of cost-control and expense cutting policies, one of which was, "Increase of operational productivity through enhancement of employees' capabilities." There was no doubt that cost-cutting was the order of the day, starting with the most obvious of places, operating-fuel burning time in Korean Air Lines' big, modern and very expensive fleet of forty-one aircraft. Every ten or twenty minutes of flying time saved by catching the right wind at the right level or by cutting corners, when accumulated, could save the company a lot of money. For example, if Flight 007 had been able to shave twenty minutes off its scheduled flying time on August 31, and, on the same day, five others of Harry Cho's fleet had managed to do the same thing (with appropriate bonuses or other incentives for their captains), the saving for the company would be in the order of $13,000. Given that the airline operates some 130 international flights every week, the opportunity for that scale of flying time and corner cutting is by no means unrealistic. The cumulative results would be in the neighbourhood of half a million dollars a month, or $6 million a year — almost the amount of Korean Air Lines' profit in 1982 after the massive losses in 1980-81. Even a one-million dollar saving, to say nothing of six million, would be a good business target.

These are good, sound, hard-driving management actions, designed to turn a company on the brink of financial disaster back into a profitable undertaking. Cost-shaving and the cutting of corners was perfectly justified, provided that there was no impingement on the company's excellent safety record.

With this kind of policy in effect, in order to save the airline and their jobs, the pilots would be very much aware of and committed to the whole concept of cost-cutting. For a senior leading pilot such as Captain Chun, who, like his boss, was aggressive and combative, it would be a matter of pride and leadership to be able to rack up a record of flying-time saving.

As a matter of reputation among members of the aviation industry, its executives and pilots, Korean Air Lines with its lower-than-low fares and its fast, debt-making growth, is recognized as being – like its leader – extremely aggressive. This aggressiveness is further evidenced by the KAL practice of, from time to time, "jumping the line" in order to save fuel and cut minutes off flying time.

To "jump the line", a pilot approaching his destination but still outside the range of the ground-control radar (about two hundred miles) will gave a false position report to the control tower advising that his aircraft is much closer to the airport than it really is. If the control tower falls for the ploy, it will then give the pilot landing priority when other aircraft are in fact ahead of him in the line-up trying to land.

The word in the industry is that the Koreans had quite a reputation for jumping the line in the past, but seem to have reformed in the last couple of years.

Even so, the Korean pilots are recognized as being persistent fuel savers, because of the airline's struggle to overcome its losses, and also because of high cost of jet fuel, all of which has to be imported into South Korea.

Notwithstanding its heavy losses in 1980-81, KAL has continued its policy of extremely low fares in order to increase its share of the passenger market. A one-way economy fare New York-Seoul-Tokyo could be as little as $938, whereas the comparable Japan Air Lines price from New York to Tokyo is about double that amount.

With fares that low, it is not surprising that Congressman Larry McDonald was prepared to wait from Sunday to Tuesday to catch the next Korean Air Lines flight when he missed the one on Sunday. There was a Pan Am flight available to him that day but, because of the fare saving, he elected to wait.

Through a United States-South Korea agreement, Korean Air Lines has the right to charge whatever fare it chooses for its trans-Pacific flights. Obviously, it takes full advantage of that privilege.

It was Korean Air Lines' close connection with the United States that made it one of the choice targets of the Soviet counter-propaganda campaign that followed the shooting down of Flight 007.

In the continuing attempt to link KAL with the Central Intelligence Agency of the United States, thereby asserting without any evidence except propaganda that Flight 007 was on an electronic spying mission on behalf of the CIA, several articles were written by Soviet "experts." The objective was to convince a gullible western press and its reading public that Korean Air Lines was nothing more than a pawn of the CIA and, of course, that the United States was the party responsible for the shooting down of the 747. Incredible as it may seem, the Soviets have been largely successful in achieving that objective through their masterful propaganda activities.

One example of the massive flow of disinformation churned out by the Russians is Colonel K. Borisov's article of September 16, published by the Western media. The headline read: "South Korean Air Lines in the service of CIA."

> In the late 1960's it (Korean Air Lines) was on the brink of bankruptcy. It was then that it came to the attention of the United States intelligence services.
>
> Washington gave it financial and material assistance and a whole series of privileges.
>
> The fact that back in the early 1970's a totally secret agreement was concluded between the U.S. Central Intelligence Agency, which reports to the President personally, and KAL, on the use of the latter's passenger

planes for conducting reconnaissance of the Soviet Union's territory is no "news" to the White House leadership. Under that agreement, several airplanes – first and foremost American-made Boeings – were specially equipped with photographic and radio devices for espionage. This was disclosed at one time by, among others, Colonel Chun Byung In of the South Korean Air Force Reserve, the captain of the crew of the South Korean Boeing 747 that intruded into the Soviet Union's airspace on the night of Sept. 1, 1983. He had boasted to close friends that he carried out special missions for American intelligence, and he had even showed some of them the espionage equipment on his plane, which would be used for reconnaissance of Soviet military facilities during flights from New York to Seoul. Regarded as one of KAL's best pilots, he had even been assigned to pilot the government's Boeing 747 during the South Korean president's trips to the United States and southeast Asian countries in 1981 and 1982. This is why attempts to portray him as a novice who strayed into "Soviet airspace" or was flying with faulty navigational and communications equipment look so absurd. It's significant, however, that, despite his seemingly successful career, Chun Byung In intended to leave the airline soon because of, as he had told close friends, the great risk to his life that performing reconnaissance missions for the CIA entailed.

This article was widely reported in the western press the next day, September 17, 1983. There was not then and there is not now any evidence to support the allegation about KAL airplanes being specially equipped with photographic and radio devices for espionage; nor about the statements and intentions attributed to Captain Chun Byung In.

After dealing with what it claimed was evidence of other ties between KAL and American intelligence services, the article closed with a grand attack on KAL and the United States, the "provocateurs":

KAL also maintains close ties to the United States along military lines. The airline's plants, which were built with assistance from the American firms, Northrop, Hughes and others, assemble F-5 fighters and combat helicopters in South Korea under American licenses. It receives economically advantageous orders for repair work on the aviation equipment of American Air Force and Navy groupings deployed in the Western Pacific.

In light of all these facts, the bare-faced lies and hypocrisy to which President Reagan and those close to him are resorting in their attempt to portray the South Korean Boeing 747's intrusion into the airspace of the Soviet Far East as "unpremeditated," "accidental" and having no connection with intelligence purposes, becomes obvious. . . .

The world public will get to the bottom of this. The provocateurs will not succeed in evading the judgment of history and their responsibility for the criminal action against the Soviet Union, its sovereign rights and its security interests.

In the last sentence is found the essence of the U.S.S.R.'s counter-attack. After stonewalling the world and refusing even to admit that it had shot down Flight 007, it would now proceed to convince the public outside the Soviet Union that it was the United States and Korean Air Lines itself that were responsible for the destruction of the 747 and the massacre of the 269 souls on board. The provocateurs — the United States and Korean Air Lines — were responsible for the criminal action against the Soviet Union because the aircraft was engaged in espionage activity for the United States.

This article and others that flowed from Moscow had the desired effect. A large segment of the public of the western world believes that Flight 007 was indeed engaged in an espionage misson for the CIA and that the United States is at fault.

These allegations have been enormously successful from a propaganda point of view. The real question is: Was Flight

007 in fact engaged in an espionage mission for the CIA? That question fits the heading: "Why was Flight 007 over Kamchatka and Sakhalin?"

Whatever the answer to that question, there is little doubt that Choong Hoon Cho, his Han Jin Group and Korean Air Lines have strong and close ties with the aviation industry of the United States and that America is one of the largest markets for not only Korean Air Lines but the entire South Korean nation.

5

SHOULD SOMEONE HAVE WARNED FLIGHT 007?

MUCH HAS BEEN said about why Flight 007 was not alerted to the fact that it was being pursued by Russian fighters.

If there had been any opportunity for the U.S. military to give a warning, that warning might have come from the RC-135 reconnaissance aircraft that had been near the 747 as it was approaching the Kamchatka Peninsula. A second possible source of a warning was from the radar or radio coverage from the U.S. Air Force base on Shemya Island, 135 miles from the Neeva checkpoint.

The RC-135 was at one point near Flight 007 (although there is no U.S. admission that there was any contact whatsoever between the two aircraft, whereas the Russians claim – without evidence – that the two rendezvoused and exchanged signals; of this there is no record) and was on its way back to the Shemya air base when the Korean airplane was over Kamchatka and being pursued. The distance from the RC-135 was probably in the neighborhood of five hundred miles and rapidly lengthening. That would be well out of the range of any radar the RC-135 reconnaissance aircraft might have had on board. Furthermore there is no evidence that the crew of the RC-135 at any time knew that they were within seventy-five miles of the Korean aircraft or that it was heading toward Kamchatka. The likelihood is that they did not have a clue that it was nearby or off course or headed for Soviet airspace. That proposition has validity unless one accepts the Soviet version that the two aircraft rendezvoused.

The version of the President of the United States has far more credibility and makes far more sense than the rendezvous scenario painted by the Soviet Armed Forces Chief of General Staff, Marshal Ogarkov, at his unprecedented press conference with western journalists on September 9, 1983. The RC-135 crew did not know the 747 was over Sakhalin. And even if someone on the reconnaissance machine was monitoring the Soviet fighter aircraft channels (assuming he could understand Russian) and heard them chattering as they pursued the "target," the American crew would not have any idea what the target was that the Russians were after.

By the time the Korean 747 reached Soviet airspace over Sakhalin Island, the RC-135 had been on the ground at Shemya for an hour. Even if another one had been airborne and on station off the Kamchatka coast, the 747 with the Soviet fighters chasing it over Sakhalin would have been hundreds of miles out of radar range and, similarly, out of VHF radio range.

Any military radar installation at Shemya would have a range of probably no more than three hundred miles, which means that it could not track the 747 either over Kamchatka or over Sakhalin Island. Nor would it be able to receive the aircraft's VHF transmissions, because Shemya would be well beyond the 150-NM range of that type of radio. Military radar might have been able to monitor any high-frequency transmissions from Flight 007 to air traffic control at Tokyo but would have heard nothing unusual. If any U.S. military radio equipment was monitoring the Anchorage air controllers' frequency it would have been on a voice-activated machine that simply recorded the transmissions. There would be no one listening.

This, of course, was the system used by the Japanese when they acquired the transmissions of the Russian fighter planes stalking Flight 007 over Sakhalin. All those transmissions were automatically recorded on Japanese voice-activated receivers. It was not until well after the destruction of the aircraft had occurred and the Japanese authorities had begun to realize what had happened that the relevant sections of the recording tape were found and the process of translation began.

To sum up, there was no way the American military knew on a real time basis either that Flight 007 was in Soviet airspace or that it was being followed and in danger of being attacked. The Japanese air controllers and military were in a somewhat different position; even so, the result turned out to be the same.

Flight 007 moved into the jurisdiction of Japanese air traffic control when it had passed Nippi and had reported that it was over that waypoint. Its report was accepted by Anchorage and by Narita, the Japanese air control center at Tokyo, as being correct. Neither control center had any reason to believe otherwise: there was no civilian radar coverage of the aircraft either at Nippi or at waypoint Nokka. The 747 crew reported waypoint passage at Nippi at 17:07, whereas in fact it was over 250 nautical miles to the northwest, flying over Sakhalin.

What happened was that the Japanese military radar operators at Wakkanai on the northern tip of the Japanese island of Hokkaido had the 747 on their screens but thought it was a Soviet transport being escorted by four interceptor aircraft. The radar operators watched the blip of the aircraft, then followed it as it plunged toward the sea. At that time they had no way of knowing it was Flight 007. Even if the military operators had been in direct touch with Japanese civilian air traffic control, they would have been told that they had no straying aircraft; that all of their flights, including Flight 007, reported that they were on their flight-planned routes outside Soviet airspace.

Furthermore, even though Flight 007 had its transponder on and was squawking SSR code 1300, this identification signal (which appeared on the radar operator's screen next to the 747's blip) failed to give any indication that the aircraft being monitored was not a Soviet machine. After all, Soviet Aeroflot and military transport airlines carry transponders for the same purposes as the rest of the world's air carriers.

An aircraft's transponder emits a coded electronic signal which gives the plane's four-digit identifying number. When the number is inserted into air traffic control (or military) computers on the ground, it will automatically appear beside the aircraft's blip on the air controller's radar.

There was no possibility of warning Flight 007 of its location deep in Soviet airspace, or that it was being pursued by Soviet interceptors. Co-pilot Sohn had been calmly giving waypoint position reports telling air traffic control that the 747 was on route R20. There was no radar to check on him and so Anchorage and Narita at Tokyo had no choice but to believe him.

And what else could the unsuspecting radar operator believe when at 18:12 he first saw the big blip well inside Soviet airspace northeast of Sakhalin Island with four smaller blips close by? It had to be a Soviet transport.

Even if there had been a warning at that late stage, what could the Flight 007 crew have done about it? Would they have taken evasive action? Would they have looked out of the cockpit windows and seen the Su-15 first on the right side, then on the left?

Or would they have ignored the warning that they were deep in Soviet airspace and being pursued?

The fact is they were not warned. The circumstances and the radar and radio facilities did not permit it.

It is reasonable to expect that the appropriate U.S., Japanese and international authorities, such as ICAO, will work together to produce a cross-checking system between military and civilian radar and radio installations along route R20 that will prevent a recurrence of the 747 massacre.

6

WHAT THE SOVIET PILOT SAW

THE FIRST Soviet response to the outcry over the shooting down of Flight 007 came on September 1 in a brief statement issued by TASS, the Soviet press agency:

> An unidentified plane entered the airspace of the Soviet Union over the Kamchatka Peninsula from the direction of the Pacific Ocean and then for the second time violated the airspace of the U.S.S.R. over Sakhalin Island on the night from August 31 to September 1. The plane did not have navigation lights, did not respond to queries and did not enter into contact with the dispatcher service.
>
> Fighters of the anti-aircraft defense, which were sent aloft toward the intruder plane, tried to give it assistance in directing it to the nearest airfield. But the intruder plane did not react to the signals and warning from the Soviet fighters and continued its flight in the direction of the Sea of Japan.

In a much longer statement issued the same day in Moscow, TASS amplified its position, saying, in part:

> It was natural that during the time the unidentified intruder plane was in the U.S.S.R. airspace, Soviet antiair defense aircraft were ordered aloft, which repeatedly tried to establish contacts with the plane using generally accepted signals and to take it to the nearest airfield in

the territory of the Soviet Union. The intruder plane, however, ignored all this. Over Sakhalin Island, a Soviet aircraft fired warning shots and tracer shells along the flying route of the plane.

Soon after this the intruder plane left the limits of Soviet airspace and continued its flight toward the Sea of Japan. For about ten minutes it was within the observation zone of radio location means, after which it could be observed no more.

As of September 2, the Soviets were not about to admit that they had shot down Flight 007. It was only when the tapes of the Soviet fighter pilot's communications with the ground during the attack were played at the United Nations by the United States that the Soviets finally capitulated.

Still later, on September 6, the Soviet government issued another statement in which it staked out its basic propaganda ground, attempting to shift the blame to the United States. For the first time it relied on the U.S. admission that an RC-135 reconnaissance aircraft had been in the area. And for the first time the Soviet government admitted that it had stopped "the actions of the intruder plane." In other words, it had shot the 747 down.

This statement said in part:

> The intruder plane entered the airspace over Kamchatka in an area where a most important base of the strategic nuclear forces of the U.S.S.R. is located. At the same time – and this is now admitted by the American side – another spy plane of the United States Air Force, an RC-135 that is similar to it, was in the same area near the Soviet border on the same altitude.
>
> Several Soviet interceptor planes were sent aloft. One of them controlled the actions of the American RC-135 plane. A second flew into the area where the intruder plane was and signaled to it that it had intruded into the airspace of the U.S.S.R. The warnings were ignored.

When it was approaching Sakhalin Island the intruder was again intercepted by fighter planes of the antiaircraft defenses. And again attempts were made to establish contact with it, including with the help of the known general call signal on the international emergency frequency of 121.5 megacycles. Contrary to the false contentions of the United States president, Soviet antiaircraft defense fighter planes are fitted out with the communication equipment in which this frequency is fixed. So these signals had to be received by the intruder plane, but it did not respond to them. Neither did it respond, as it has been said earlier, also to other signals and actions of the Soviet fighter planes.

The Soviet radio control services picked up short coded radio signals transmitted from time to time, such signals that [are] usually used in transmitting intelligence information.

The antiaircraft forces command of the area, having analyzed thoroughly the actions of the intruder plane, its route passing also in the area of Sakhalin over military bases, arrived at the conclusion that a reconnaissance aircraft performing special tasks was in the airspace of the U.S.S.R. We arrived at this conclusion also because of the fact that the plane was flying over strategically important areas of the Soviet Union. The fighter plane made warning shots with tracer shells along the route of the intruder plane. Such a measure is envisaged by international rules.

Since even after this the intruder plane did not obey the demand to fly to a Soviet airfield and tried to evade pursuit, the interceptor-fighter plane of the antiaircraft defences fulfilled the order of the command post to stop the flight. Such actions are fully in keeping with the law on the state border of the U.S.S.R., which has been published.

The Soviet pilots, in stopping the actions of the intruder plane, could not know that it was a civilian aircraft. It was flying without navigation lights at the height of night in conditions of bad visibility and was not answering the signals. The assertions of the United States president that Soviet pilots knew that it was a civilian aircraft are not in keeping with reality.

It is seldom that one can find so many false statements and so much disinformation in seven relatively short paragraphs.

The RC-135 is not similar to the 747, either in size or shape. No Soviet interceptor controlled the actions of the American RC-135 plane, which at all times was outside Soviet airspace.

No Soviet fighter found KAL's 747 over Kamchatka and therefore no signals were made to it there that it had intruded into the airspace of the U.S.S.R. A warning not given cannot be ignored.

On most versions of the transcripts of the taped conversations of the Soviet pilots with their ground control there is no evidence that any attempt was made by them to make a general call signal on the international emergency frequency of 121.5 megacycles.

On the other hand, the transcript attached as Appendix D to the final report of the ICAO investigation team had a different translation than that issued by the U.S. government on the transmission at 18:13:26 which was:

"805. The target isn't responding to I.F.F. (Identification/Friend or Foe)."

The ICAO version was:

"805. The target isn't responding to the call."

If the ICAO version was correct then what "call" was the Su-15 pilot referring to? Was it a call he had made at 121.5 megacycles? And if so, had he made it in English, the international language of the air?

This is the only glimmer of evidence to support the claim of an attempt to contact on 121.5 megacycles. And there is no claim by the Soviets that their Su-15 pilot could speak English.

Furthermore the ICAO transcript is defective because it is a version that was not corrected by the revised translations issued by the U.S. on September 11. The main revision, of course, was the change of "I have broken off lock-on" at 18:20:49 to "I am firing cannon bursts."

If the ICAO investigation team made similar errors in conducting its inquiry, there must be serious doubt as to the accuracy and value of its conclusions.

Under the circumstances the "I.F.F." translation is much more credible than the ICAO's "call". The conclusion must be that there is no evidence that a call was made by the Su-15 pilot to the KAL 747 on 121.5 megacycles.

The Soviet fighters that intercepted the Korean jet used an emergency guard channel in a very high frequency that is preset on the ground and cannot be tuned by the pilot once his aircraft is airborne. This frequency is not compatible with the 121.5 or 243.0 megacycles guard channels used by commercial and military aircraft of the west. This is to preclude defection by Soviet pilots. Therefore, Flight 007 could not respond to a signal it had not received.

Moreover, while the Su-15 with 805 at the controls was first abeam the 747, then to the right of it and then to the left, there was no indication from the tapes that the pilot attempted to make any of the navigation-light flicking and wing-rocking signals required in accordance with the standards for interception laid down by ICAO. Those rules will be explained below.

The short coded radio signals cited by TASS were probably transmissions from the 747 to Japanese air traffic control at Narita.

The firing of warning shots with tracer shells along the route of the intruder plane is not a measure envisaged by international rules, although it was by a Soviet government air defense law.

Article 36 of the Soviet Border Law, created in November 1982 directs:

> Use weapons and military technology for repulsing armed attack and invasion of Soviet territory, for suppressing armed provocations on the border . . . and

also against violators of the state border of the U.S.S.R. on land, water and in the air, in response to the use of force by them or in cases when stopping the violation cannot be achieved by other means.

The gist of Article 36 as applied in the Flight 007 case is, "Use weapons when stopping the border violation cannot be achieved by other means."

There was no demand to fly to a Soviet airfield communicated to the Korean flight crew by the flashing of lights, by radio contact, or by other means. Flight 007 made no attempt to evade pursuit and the reduction of speed that concerned the Soviet fighter pilot was simply the result of the 747's beginning to climb to another altitude after obtaining approval from Japanese air traffic control.

The Soviet pilot who fired the rockets must have known that the aircraft was a Boeing 747 and that it was carrying civilian markings. The Su-15 pilot said, "After observing the maneuvers of the plane, I became convinced it was either a spy plane or a different kind of bomber." If he could see the maneuvers, he could see the airplane and knew what it was without any doubt. It was not flying without navigation lights. It had on both navigation and flashing red warning beacons, as the Soviet fighter pilot reported several times to his controller, Deputat. The visibility was not bad; rather, it was clear with the light of almost a half moon.

The end of the long text of the statement by the Soviet government on September 6 concluded with two paragraphs that again clearly stated the objective of the Soviet propaganda campaign – a campaign that on September 6, was just beginning to gather steam. The objective was to convince the world that even though the Soviets had shot down the Korean 747 and killed its 269 people in cold blood, it was really the United States of America that was responsible for the massacre:

The people on the plane that was used by American

special services for their dirty games fell victim to a fresh crime.

The Soviet government expresses regret over the death of innocent people and shares the sorrow of their bereaved relatives and friends. The entire responsibility for this tragedy rests wholly and fully with the leaders of the United States of America.

Notwithstanding the provisions of the Soviets' new "border law" (Article 36), which outline the circumstances in which intruding aircraft should be shot down, ICAO guidelines set a three-phase procedure, which the Soviet fighter pilot ought to have followed, for identifying an aircraft.

1. An interceptor should approach its target from astern, taking a position on the port side of the aircraft and at the same level, within view of the pilot of the intercepted aircraft and no closer than one thousand feet.

2. The interceptor should close in gently to identify the aircraft. (The Soviet fighter pilot did this and identified the aircraft. He made no report to Deputat because he was not asked to do so; nor was it his duty as a Soviet fighter pilot to identify an aircraft that had already been designated a spy reconnaissance aircraft by the authorities on the ground.)

3. After identification, the interceptor should break away in a shallow dive.

All other intercepting aircraft are to remain well clear. During this procedure, the interceptor command pilot is instructed to use visual signals that the aircraft is being intercepted, and interceptor ground control and the interceptor should make an attempt to reach the intercepted aircraft on 121.5 megacycles. (There is no evidence from the tapes that the pilot gave any visual signal, except that he fired his cannon; and it is not known whether he fired those cannon shells *at* the aircraft or if they were tracers used as a signal. Neither the ground control nor the pilot made an attempt to reach the aircraft on 121.5 megacycles. None of the commercial airliners in the area, including Flight 015, heard any transmissions on 121.5 during the intercept period.)

The rules also stress that close co-ordination should be maintained by intercept ground control and air traffic services.

The ICAO procedures for aircraft that have been intercepted are as follows:

– Follow instruction given by the intercepting aircraft.
– Notify appropriate air traffic services.
– Identify your aircraft and describe the nature of the flight, using the emergency frequency 121.5 MHz. If no contact has been established, repeat the call on frequency 243 MHz.
– If your aircraft is equipped with a radar transponder, select Mode A Code 7700 unless otherwise instructed by air traffic services.

Signaling procedures between an interceptor and an intercepted aircraft are:

– Day: Interceptor rocks wings from a position in front and normally to the left of the intercepted aircraft. After acknowledgement from the intercepted aircraft, which also rocks its wings, the interceptor goes into a slow, level turn to a desired heading. The other aircraft is to follow.
– Night: The interceptor follows the same procedure as day and adds flashing navigational lights at regular intervals. The intercepted aircraft also flashes navigational lights.

Except as previously discussed, there is no evidence on the tapes that the Soviet interceptor flashed his navigation lights at regular intervals, or that he flashed them at all. The only attempt at signaling (if it was indeed signaling rather than an attempt to destroy the aircraft) was the firing of the four bursts of cannon shells, some or all of which were tracer – that is, they burned with a brilliant light as they burst through the sky. To fire four bursts of, say, thirty cannon shells each would mean that each burst lasted no more than one or two seconds. The trajectory of a high-velocity cannon shell of the caliber carried in the Su-15 fighter aircraft would rapidly curve downward as it lost speed once it was at its maximum range of one kilometer from the point of firing. Assuming that the Soviet fighter pilot was able to perfectly place the tracer shells parallel to the path of the 747 either on the right or the left of it, and that the tracer shells went by the aircraft at a level slightly above the jumbo jet, so that the pilots could see them out of the corners of their eyes, the 747 pilots might well have seen one or all of the four bursts, all of which would have been let off in rapid succession.

On the other hand, if both the pilots had been in a "heads down" position checking the instruments or reading a map or chart, or if the shells passed below the restricted downward line of sight that the pilots have out of each side of the aircraft (their seats are well in from the windows), the pilots would not have seen the tracers. Furthermore, four to eight seconds is an extremely short period of time.

In my opinion, when the Soviet fighter pilot fired his cannon he was attempting to destroy the Boeing 747 and had been ordered to do so by his ground control. Either he failed to hit the target or, if he did hit it, he could see that he was not going to bring it down. That is why, only two minutes and forty-eight seconds after he reported, "I am firing cannon bursts," he said, "Now I will try rockets."

Whatever the Soviet pilot's intentions, and despite the claims of the Soviet government, the firing of tracer shells from a cannon is not a procedure provided for in the international interception rules. Nor is there any provision for "warning shots." In fact, if Captain Chun, an experienced former fighter pilot with the South Korean Air Force, had suddenly seen tracer shells blasting past close to his aircraft, he might well have believed that he was being fired at. Instinctively he would have immediately started violent evasive action. Instead the 747 moved straight on, starting its climb from 33,000 feet to 35,000. Captain Chun took no action whatsoever, which doubtless means that he never saw the tracers from the Su-15. He continued on his course at 240 degrees.

The slowing down of the 747 in the climb was interpreted

by the Soviet pilot as an evasion "trick that is often used by U.S. pilots manning RC-135's." He also claimed that the KAL pilot lowered the 747's flaps to reduce its speed quickly, so the interceptor would overshoot it and have to turn around before making another approach, thereby giving the airliner time to escape. "But I did not fall for that trick," the Su-15 pilot boasted.

Nor can anyone fall for the Soviet pilot's claim, because if the flaps had been lowered at the aircraft's cruising speed of some 540 nautical miles an hour, they would have been ripped off.

What is clear from the tapes of the Soviet pilot's conversation with his ground control is that, even though he was abeam the 747, first on the right, then on the left, he made no attempt to flash his navigational lights at regular intervals as required by ICAO procedure. This talkative pilot would have reported that step if he had taken it, just as he reported the firing of the cannon. Also there is no evidence that the Soviet fighter had its navigational lights on, in which case the crew of the 747 would likely not have seen it in the darkness, even with the moonlight.

While dealing with the matters of interception, signalling, warnings and the claims of evasion, there is one other significant claim made by the Soviets that can be examined here. Marshal Ogarkov dealt with it in the opening statement of his famous, unprecedented press conference of September 9. This is the claim that the 747 "sharply altered its course." Here is the Marshal's statement:

> The third stage. The actions in this stage became defiant. No matter what attempts to contact it were made, it did not respond to signals from Soviet interceptor planes. Moreover, it began to maneuver, changing its speed and altitude of flight, obviously trying to evade the Soviet airplane. [It changed its altitude commencing at 18:20 some eighteen minutes after what the Marshal describes next.] It is characteristic that at 6:02, 18:02 local time, the intruder, as can be seen on

the chart, sharply altered its course and again approached positions of our antiair defense forces base. There was no doubt then that it was a reconnaissance plane. When the plane was over the southwestern portion of the peninsula, the final attempt was made to force the plane down.

Four rounds of warning shots were fired. One hundred and twenty cartridges were fired; however, the plane did not yield to these signals but tried to evade in the general direction of Vladivostok at 6:24 local time, when it was ordered at that specific point to cut short the flight of the plane using heat-tracing missiles.

Did the intruder, as Ogarkov claimed, sharply alter its course at 18:02; or did it constantly maintain its course of 240 degrees parallel to its original flight-planned route, as President Reagan had stated?

Again the answer is found in the tape of the Russian pilot's radio transmissions and also in the map that the Soviets produced on September 2, to which Ogarkov referred (see photo section). The Soviet map traces the route of the 747 across the Sea of Okhotsk on a course that would be perhaps about 230 degrees. The route then makes a sharp right turn to a heading of 300 degrees. The alleged turnpoint at 18:02 puts the 747 on the 300-degree course for about 125 miles; then the aircraft is shown beginning a slow turn back to its original course of 230 degrees, completing one-half of the turn over the eastern edge of Sakhalin Island and straightening out as it crosses the western edge.

The distance from the beginning of the turn at 18:02 to the eastern edge of Sakhalin Island is roughly 150 miles. Let us say that the 747 would be steering a course of 300 degrees for 125 miles after it completed its 18:02 turn. That would be roughly twelve minutes of flying time at the 300-degree course, which would take the time to about 18:17. Then there would be the slow turn to the left, running the aircraft's course gradually from 300 degrees back to its original course of 240 degrees or, as the Russian map shows, 230. The distance from the eastern edge of Sakhalin Island to the point of destruction as shown on the map is about 150 miles. The time to cover that distance would be another twelve minutes, at which point – 18:26 – the aircraft is destroyed.

Let us follow the Ogarkov scenario. At 18:02 the aircraft begins its turn "sharply." Assuming that the aircraft completes its seventy-degree turn to the right in one minute and is therefore on the 300-degree course by 18:03. It will stay on that course till 18:15.

At 18:05:53, 805 reports that he is following the target on course 240.

That was the course the 747 had in fact been following since it left Bethel; it is basically the Great Circle Route from Anchorage to Seoul.

Three seconds later, at 18:05:56, 805 says, "I see it!"

He sees Flight 007 while he is flying on course 240. In the Ogarkov version the 747 is flying on a 300-degree course.

At 18:08:06, 805 acknowledges that he will "carry out course 260," then says, "on course 220 . . . 7,500 (meters)."

At 18:09:00, 805 says, "Yes, it has turned . . . . The target is 80 degrees to my left."

From the remainder of the tape it is apparent that the 747 did not turn, but that the pilot thought it had. He is now told to get behind the aircraft and follow it from a line-astern position, because at 18:09:35, just thirty-five seconds later, he says, "Executing 240," and nine seconds after that he again says, "Course 240 . . . . Roger."

At 18:13:05, 805 says, "I see it. I'm locked on to the target." This means he is directly behind the 747 and following its same course. Thirty seconds later, he reports, "The target's course is 240 degrees," and at 18:15:08, when, in the Ogarkov scenario, the 747 is still flying on the 300-degree course and about to begin its turn to the left, the man who was there in the sky tracking the 747 says, "The target's course is still the same . . . 240."

Either Marshal Nikolai V. Ogarkov, Chief of the Soviet General Staff, was deliberately lying, or he had been totally misinformed by his staff. Certainly the western press and public were misinformed. The better word is lied-to. They had been lied to by the Soviet government from its opening TASS statement on September 1, when it said the Korean 747 it had just shot down had "continued its flight in the direction of the Sea of Japan." As the American ambassador to the United Nations, Jeane Kirkpatrick, was to say, "The Soviet Union decided to shoot down a civilian airliner, shot it down and then lied about it."

7

THE SOVIET SIDE OF THE EVENT

WHAT IS THE Sukhoi Su-15 and its origins? What kind of pilot was at the controls when it shot down the KAL 747? What kind of military organization was supporting and directing the Su-15? What is in the Soviet Far East that the Russians are so anxious to hide from the United States and its allies?

The last question is the engine for the other three and, for that matter, for the entire process that brought about the 747 massacre.

Because of the enormous expansion of its military forces in the Far East region, Moscow, paranoid about the defense of the Motherland at the best of times, is doubly paranoid about the penetration of its Kamchatka, Kuril, Sea of Okhotsk and Sakhalin Island sector by foreign aircraft, particularly under the cover of darkness.

The Russians have been steadily building up their conventional military forces and their intercontinental ballistic missile installations there since the early 1970's. They have been carrying on many of their activities at night in order to conceal, as much as possible, their violations of both the SALT treaties they had entered into with the United States.

Their military building and development programs have been accomplished by means of *maskirovka*, or concealment.

The Far East strength of the Soviets, ostensibly to contain the Chinese, has upwards of 500,000 troops, 1,100 combat helicopters, 15,000 battle tanks and 3,200 combat and transport aircraft. During the past two years, both Japanese and U. S. intelligence have reported the substantial expansion of air and naval power on Sakhalin Island, and on the island of Etorofu in the Kuril Island chain about 150 miles to the north of Hokkaido. A new regiment of MiG-23's was deployed there in mid-summer 1983, complementing a major show of Soviet power toward the nearby Japanese that includes an army headquarters, a squadron of MiG-21's and an air-assault brigade with HIP and HIND helicopters.

At the Dolinsk-Sokol airbase, one of two on Sakhalin Island, there are thirty Su-15's, in addition to at least one regiment of MiG-23's.

Of major importance to the Soviets are the four naval bases in the region. The main headquarters of the Soviet Pacific fleet is at Vladivostok at the most southern tip of the Soviet mainland sector abutting China. The Russian navy has significant shipbuilding and repair facilities there. Submarines and destroyers are based at Sovetskaya Gavan, also a mainland port. The naval port allegedly overflown by Flight 007 is at the southern end of Sakhalin Island. Until a few months ago, before the destruction of the 747, this was a minor naval base augmented by a small airport. But intelligence reports indicate that the recent expansion at Corsikov has been going on at a greater rate than at any other naval installation in the region.

The other naval port allegedly overflown by Flight 007 is Petropavlovsk, on the eastern coast of the Kamchatka Peninsula, where nuclear submarines are deployed and a number of naval air bases are located.

Many of the Soviet's Pacific Fleet of twenty-five nuclear-missile submarines, when deployed into the eastern Pacific, normally must pass from the Sea of Okhotsk through the narrow La Pérouse Strait en route to or from their stations (see Map 10:1, p. 117). The strait is particularly important to the Soviets because, in the event of an emergency requiring the transiting of the fleet into the Pacific, the U.S. military could stop or impede the fleet's movement by sowing mines across the strait by aircraft. The result is that the Soviets have strengthened the air defenses on Sakhalin Island by increasing the number of planes there. An army division and substantial numbers of antiaircraft guns and surface-to-air missiles have also been placed on the island.

The Soviet Pacific fleet has an additional ninety-five nuclear- and diesel-powered submarines, an antisubmarine warfare (ASW) aircraft carrier and eighty-five cruisers, destroyers and other major surface war vessels.

The build-up on Sakhalin Island and on the Kuril Islands is part of a Soviet strategy to make the Sea of Okhotsk a secure sanctuary for Delta-class ballistic missile submarines whose SLBM's (submarine-launched ballistic missiles) can reach western targets in North America.

The Kamchatka Peninsula is one of the Soviet Union's most sensitive areas because of the build-up there of its strategic missiles. There is an infrastructure for the installation of a large number of mobile missiles at Chukotskiy on the northern tip of Kamchatka. SS-20 ICBMs (intercontinental ballistic missiles) could reach half of the United States, while the SS-16's and PL-5's at Chukotskiy have sufficient range to cover any part of the United States and Canada. When completed in that barren, remote section of the world, the Chukotskiy installation will deploy at least 115 multi-warheaded ICBMs aimed at American and Canadian cities, military and industrial installations and other targets.

The testing of the PL-5 ICBMs is done mostly at night to hamper the American ability to monitor the activity of the missiles and their points of impact. Control of these activities is under the Chief Directorate of Strategic Maskirovka, the concealment agency created by Marshal Ogarkov. (Ogarkov is now also First Deputy Minister of Defense, second only to Marshal Ustinov.)

In addition to these activities, the Soviets carry on their anti-ballistic missile (ABM) testing in the southern region of the Kamchatka Peninsula, notwithstanding the prohibition of such tests by a 1972 annex to the SALT I Agreement. As well, the Soviets have installed on Kamchatka ABM radar with full operational capability designed to guard their Far East strategic installations.

Taking all these factors into consideration, when Korean Flight 007 penetrated Soviet airspace in the early morning hours of September 1, catching the Soviets by surprise during the darkness when much of their build-up activity was going on under *maskirovka*, the reaction could be expected to be dramatic. The doubly paranoid Soviet air commanders, under possible penalty of death if they failed, would attempt to find and destroy the intruder, spy plane, bomber or whatever it was.

THERE WAS yet another important factor at work on the night of August 31-September 1 when Flight 007 moved steadily and unswervingly through Soviet airspace over the most sensitive areas in the Far East.

That factor was psychological conditioning. There is constant strain and pressure on the air commanders, pilots and radar operators who man and make up the Soviet Union's front-line air defense. They believe that the Americans might launch a massive attack against them at any time and that their spy planes and fighter bombers regularly test and sometimes penetrate Soviet airspace from bases in Japan, the Aleutians and Alaska.

The extent of the American probing and thrusting against Soviet airspace in the Far East was outlined in a public statement on September 5 by Colonel-General Semyon Romanov, chief of the main headquarters staff of air defense. According to Romanov, U.S. military aircraft had violated Soviet airspace over the Kuril Islands alone at least nine times in 1983 up to that date. He also said that there had been more violations in the Bering Strait on a line between the Soviet mainland and Alaska.

This was stressed during the state television interview with three of the pilots who had taken part in the interception of Flight 007. The television reporter, Aleksandr Tikhomirov said, "American reconnaissance aircraft constantly play on the nerves of our Air Defense Forces." He reported that pilots on Sakhalin Island sometimes flew as many as ten sorties a day to head off U.S. military aircraft. His television story had film of Su-15 fighters, their white missiles under their wings, scrambling to intercept what Tikhomirov called yet another American challenge to Soviet defenses.

Adding to these constant operational strains is a command system that integrates a direct and tight central control from headquarters in Moscow, with standing orders that make regional and local commanders open to severe punishment, even death, if intruding aircraft are allowed to escape.

Another factor adding to the strain that would affect the decision-maker's judgment on how to handle Flight 007 is, of course, the question of how that commander is going to interpret Article 36 (referred to earlier). That ordinance, promulgated in 1982, set down in no uncertain terms when weapons should be used to terminate the flight of an intruder into the sacred airspace of the Soviet Motherland.

Thus, when Captain Chun and his co-pilot, Sohn, first entered Soviet airspace over the Kamchatka Peninsula, they were taking their aircraft and all the innocent souls on board into two areas of sensitivity – sensitive military men, sensitive military installations. The result was a cruel act of the utmost *in*sensitivity. Flight 007 was about to fly over sovereign Soviet soil on which the U.S.S.R.'s most secret military and missile installations were located; and it was flying into airspace defended by men whose duty and responsibility was to be highly alert to any air intrusion and to terminate that intrusion with weapons if necessary.

Even if Captain Chun knew and understood the depths of Soviet sensitivity in this area, he was probably not aware of the existence, or the implications, of the new Soviet law, Article 36. Notwithstanding the shooting down of the KAL 707 in 1978, would he really have thought that the Soviets would commit the ultimate act of insensitivity, the destruction of the 747 and all the people in it, rather than escort his aircraft out of Soviet airspace or, at worst, force him to land?

But land where? There was no place on Sakhalin Island to

which the intruder could be led under ICAO rules. To bring a foreign military or civilian aircraft into the Dolinsk-Sokol air base or any other air base on that island would be to violate the security of that airfield and the impenetrable cloak of secrecy the Soviets had thrown over Sakhalin Island. It is closed to foreigners, and even to Soviet tourists. To have the secret sights of the Sakhalin air base exposed to the eyes of a foreign air crew, to say nothing of a planeload of passengers, would be unthinkable.

So the only alternatives for the Soviet air commander responsible for making the decisions as Flight 007 coursed through Soviet airspace were clear. After intercepting the intruder – which was essential – then the interceptor must either escort the aircraft out of Soviet airspace in accordance with ICAO regulations, or shoot it down in accordance with Article 36.

It should be noted that when the Su-15 pilot, with at least one attendant MiG-23, made the interception, Flight 007 was on course 240, which would have had it exiting Soviet airspace in about thirty minutes. The aircraft was destroyed when it was still on that course and about two minutes away from exiting.

The responsible Soviet air commander on the ground could have met his nation's ICAO responsibility by ordering his fighters to escort the 747 out, and then could have filed a stern complaint with the government of South Korea and with ICAO.

Alternatively, the Soviet commander could follow the law of his nation's Article 36 and shoot the intruder down. The decision-maker would know where his responsibility lay. It was to the law of his own land and to those above him in the hierarchy of the military and government, even if there were only one or two men in the entire Soviet Union to whom he had to report.

The Su-15 that took off in the early morning hours of September 1 from the Sakhalin Island base of Dolinsk-Sokol to destroy the intruder was an aircraft of the Voyska Protivovozdushnoy Oborony (PVO) (or The Troops of the

National Air Defense Forces [ADF]). Its commander controlled an extensive all-fronts network of 6,000 radar installations, some 3,000 fighter interceptors and more than 12,000 surface-to-air missiles (SAM).

The ADF (or Voyska PVO) is not part of the Soviet Air Force.

In the Soviet system there are five forces. The Land Forces, the Air Force and the Navy have commanders-in-chief who are in effect administrative heads and not responsible for operational control of their forces. It is their responsibility to improve and develop their services and to ensure that they are properly equipped and manned.

On the other hand, the commanders-in-chief of the Air Defense Forces and the Rocket Forces have both operational control of their forces in action and administrative responsibility.

The difference was created so that, in combat, the Air Defense Forces would operate in complete independence of any of the other forces. It follows that the commanders-in-chief of these two services report directly to the Soviet Supreme Commander, whereas the other three, because they can only operate in close conjunction, report to a combined command structure which is in place to give operational control to that structure independently of their commanders-in-chief.

In operational terms, the ADF has a central command post at Kalinin, near Moscow, under a commander-in-chief, Marshal of Aviation, A.I. Koldunov. Under him are his two major National Air Defense districts, Moscow and Baku. The remainder of the Soviet Union is divided into National Air Defense regions. It was the commander of the Biya region to whom Marshal Ogarkov attributed the decision to shoot down the KAL 747. The validity of that attribution will be a matter for discussion later in this book, when the questions of who gave the order and of why the 747 was in Soviet airspace will be discussed.

In any event, the chain of command is clear: from the ADF commander-in-chief, to the Far East commander (all forces), to the regional commanders, direct to the ADF regiments, including the ADF regiment of Su-15's at Dolinsk-Sokol; and also to the radar control unit at Deputat through which the Biya regional commander had the order to shoot passed to the Su-15 pilot with his missiles locked on to the 747.

In reverse, the chain of command and communications is: direct from the regional commander at Biya, to the Far East commander at Khabarovsk, to the ADF headquarters of the commander-in-chief in Moscow. In turn, he is subordinate only to the Chief of General Staff, Marshal Ogarkov. Ogarkov reports to the Minister of Defense – Marshal Ustinov at the time of the incident.

At the low end of the scale, the Biya regional commander had available to carry out his orders the pilot (code-named 805) in his Su-15 jet and the radar flight-control unit, Deputat.

Little is known about the pilot except what was gleaned from the television interview, with reporter Aleksandr Tikhomirov, that was released to the western world on September 10.

From the television program, "805" appears to be around forty years of age, a little heavy around the jowls, with bushy brown hair. Altogether, a not-unpleasant-looking man. (See photo section.) From the sound of his voice on the tapes and his appearance on the television program, he might be described as a "cool customer" who knew exactly what he was doing. At an advanced age for a fighter pilot he is obviously highly experienced and probably of senior rank, perhaps a Lieutenant-Colonel. He might even be the commander of the Su-15 regiment at Dolinsk-Sokol.

This transcript of what he said during the television interview may provide a better insight into the man:

> When he cut into our airspace I knew it was an enemy, an enemy who stole into other's airspace, flying over my house –actually he didn't fly over our base strictly speaking – on a spying mission.

I approached the plane and I flashed my navigation lights. Incidentally, on a Boeing 747 the crew is quite large. They should have seen the signals. We can find out. We can verify that.

Right in front of him I fired four rounds of tracer heating bullets.

And then I rocked my wings. He must have seen me.

This signified in code, "You're an intruder." He had to answer somehow that, "Yes, I'm an intruding aircraft and in trouble," and I would have helped him, if he was in trouble; and if he was an intruder he could have landed on our airfield and we would have sorted it out.

But he kept flying on the same course and at the same altitude, and I received a command, a precise and definite command.

The command was to destroy the target.

The fighter airplane 805 was flying – and presumably he had been flying this same type for many years – is the Sukhoi Su-15, known in the West as the Flagon (see photo section). The first Flagon A version entered ADF service in 1969. There are some seven hundred Su-15 Flagons in the ADF's inventory, from the Flagon A version through to the F, as technological changes and advances have been made to constantly up-date the machine over the years.

The aircraft has two afterburning single-shaft turbo jets; these are believed to be the Lyulka AL7F, with 22,046 pounds of thrust each. The wingspan is only 34 feet 6 inches against a length of 68 feet. The estimated maximum speed, at altitude with two missiles, is 1520 MPH (2445 Km/H, Mach 2.3). The initial climb to 35,000 feet (10,670 meters) takes one minute. The service ceiling is 65,000 feet and the aircraft has a combat radius of 450 miles.

For armanent, two underwing pylons normally carry one radar-guided "ANAB" missile and one heat-seeking infra-red "ANAB," each with seventy-pound warheads (see Figure

7:1). Two pylons under the fuselage normally carry drop tanks, but in this instance carried a 23 mm GSh-23 two-barrel cannon between them. The name ANAB, like the name Flagon, was assigned by NATO for its own purposes and is not a name used by the Soviets.

The later E and F aircraft, of which 805's machine was undoubtedly one, are equipped with the Twin Scan and Foxfire state-of-the-art radar systems, which 805 would have used to track down the 747 ahead of him. The Foxfire radar locks on to the target aiming the fighter aircraft and its ANAB missiles. The radar-guided ANAB has a range of twelve miles, while the infra-red heat-seeking missile has a range of half that distance, at six miles.

The Flagon's combat radius of 450 miles is extremely short because of its limited fuel capacity. At a low supersonic speed of, say, nine hundred miles an hour, it would be out of fuel in half an hour. With the cannons slung underneath it there would be no drop tank to provide extra fuel. Therefore

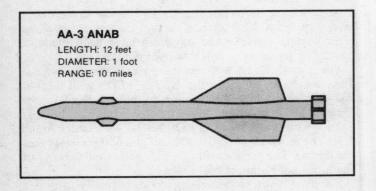

AA-3 ANAB

LENGTH: 12 feet
DIAMETER: 1 foot
RANGE: 10 miles

Figure 7:1   The Su-15's rocket.

pilot 805 was quite concerned about the amount of fuel he had left. At 18:26:53, exactly twenty-one minutes after his first recorded transmission and thirty-one seconds after advising Deputat, "The target is destroyed," 805 reported, "Fuel remainder 1,600." He had 1,600 liters, or 423 gallons, left. At subsonic speed that amount would get him back to his base with a reasonable reserve.

Both the aircraft and its pilot had done the job they were sent up to do – destroy the target – and they had done it with cold efficiency.

8

THE RC-135 FACTOR

THE INFUSION of the United States Air Force electronic intelligence (ELINT) aircraft, the RC-135, into the aftermath boiling pot was probably the major propaganda advantage handed to the Soviets in their vigorous word-assault on the United States. A second most important advantage was given to them when the Americans corrected the interpretation of the tape recording of the Soviet pilot's air-to-ground reports, admitting that the Su-15 pilot had in fact stated that he was firing his cannon.

The Soviets had begun their response to world charges that they had shot down Flight 007 by two TASS statements on September 1 and 2. The first was brief and said that the aircraft "continued its flight in the direction of the Sea of Japan." The second was a lengthy claim that the aircraft had violated Soviet airspace when it spent more than two hours over the Kamchatka Peninsula, the Sea of Okhotsk and the Island of Sakhalin. This opening shot indicated the direction in which the Soviet propaganda thrust would move: in the Soviet version, the intrusion of the 747 was a preplanned act with special intelligence aims. Three sequential paragraphs signal the Soviet intention to shift the blame onto the United States:

> In the light of these facts the intrusion into the airspace by the mentioned plane cannot be regarded in any other way than [as] a preplanned act. It was obviously thought possible to attain special intelligence gains without hindrance using civilian planes as a cover.

More than that, there is reason [to believe] that those who organized this provocation had deliberately desired a further aggravation of the international situation, striving to smear the Soviet Union, to sow hostility to it and to cast aspersions on the Soviet peace-loving policy.

This is illustrated also by the impudent, slanderous statement in respect of the Soviet Union that was instantly made by President Reagan of the United States.

There are two points to be noted here. The first is that the Soviets had, in effect, denied that they had shot down the KAL 747.

The second is that there was no mention of any involvement of an RC-135 aircraft being in the area of the 747's flight path approaching Kamchatka, or of any rendezvous. It is reasonable to expect that, if the Soviets knew on September 2 of the RC-135's presence, they would have said so on that day, because they were grasping for every straw blowing by.

The first mention by the Soviets of an RC-135 was on September 4. The claim was not that an RC-135 was involved, but rather that a Soviet fighter pilot could have mistaken the airliner for the reconnaissance plane.

On September 3, TASS issued another lengthy statement intensifying its allegations that the United States was ultimately responsible for the 747 being shot down. It claimed that the White House was carrying on a worldwide, rabid anti-Soviet campaign over the affair. There was still no admission that the Soviets had shot the aircraft down. And there was still no reference to the involvement of an RC-135.

The claim was made by Colonel-General Semyon F. Romanov, chief of the main headquarters staff of the ADF, in comments to Soviet newsmen, quoted by TASS, in which he said the 747 "flew with extinguished lights, and its outlines resemble much those of the American reconnaissance plane

RC-135." (See photo section for comparison of the 747 and the RC-135.)

On Saturday, September 3, TASS quoted not a Soviet source but an Australian newspaper, *The Sydney Morning Herald*, which had given the opinion that the 747 "could have been taken in the Soviet Union for a spy plane, since on radars it looks like an intelligence plane of the U.S. Air Force, "and that it "could also well be mistaken for a U.S. E4B bomber."

However there was still no Moscow claim that the ADF's radar or interceptor aircraft had spotted another plane.

Apparently Romanov and ADF headquarters in Moscow did not know the RC-135 had been tracked by the Kamchatka radar. For that matter, it could well be that the radar operators on the Kamchatka Peninsula did not see the RC-135 and the 747 on their screens when they were in the same area because they were possibly out of radar range. Or, if the operators did see them, the two aircraft were in reality so far apart – a minimum distance of seventy-five miles, according to U.S. officials – that it was not an unusual incident and not worth reporting.

On the same day that General Romanov made his statement, but after it was published, the Reagan Administration, through its officials, stated that an American reconnaissance plane, an RC-135 that was operating off the Siberian coast the night the South Korean airliner was downed, was on a routine mission and was unaware that the Korean plane had entered Soviet airspace or was in trouble. It was stated that the RC-135 was 1,000 miles away from the area where the South Korean 747 was at the time it was destroyed.

In a report datelined Washington, September 4, the *New York Times* said:

> Rejecting Soviet assertions that the reconnaissance plane violated Soviet airspace, the officials said the American plane flew no closer than 50 miles from the Soviet coastline, apparently in reference to the Kam-

chatka Peninsula, and was in international not Soviet airspace.

It is strange that U.S. officials would be "rejecting Soviet assertions," because to that point there had been no public Soviet assertions whatsoever. And since the Soviets were making all of their statements in public, it is doubtful that they raised any complaints with the United States without letting the world know as well.

Perhaps the Reagan Administration officials had misread the Romanov statement and thought it contained a violation allegation, which it did not. Or perhaps the Presidency decided that the public should know all the facts and that the RC-135 information as of that date would have no effect or bearing on the situation as it was developing in the propaganda war between the Soviets and the United States.

Whatever the reason, the Reagan people let the cat out of the bag that the Soviets may well not have known about at all. They certainly had not mentioned it when they were throwing every brick at the United States they could put their hands on. On Sunday, September 4, President Reagan invited congressional leaders of both parties to the White House to brief them about the Korean Air Lines' Flight 007 incident and to advise them of the presence of the RC-135.

Sensing that the RC-135 information should have been kept under wraps, the minority leader, Senator Robert C. Byrd of West Virginia, said after the briefing, "I'm sorry it was even mentioned. It is not pertinent at all to the situation. It has confused the situation, and it need not. The Soviets cannot hide behind it."

The Soviets would not only hide behind it, they would drape the RC-135's presence like a flag around themselves to demonstrate their innocence and show they had every right to believe that the intruder was on an espionage mission.

The next day, September 5, in preparation for President Reagan's national television address scheduled that night for

8:00 p.m., a statement was read to reporters at the White House about the presence of the RC-135 in the vicinity of Flight 007. This statement put the Soviets in an excellent position. They now had information about an event that apparently they themselves had no record of, at least up until Sunday, September 4. The Americans laid it all out for them. All the Russians had to do was fabricate a rendezvous between Flight 007 and the RC-135, and they had a propaganda device that would convince a large part of the western world that the two aircraft did in fact rendezvous, that they were linked electronically and that the 747 was indeed on an espionage mission.

These are the relevant parts of the statement that would become the major propaganda battleground between the two superpowers:

A U.S. RC-135 aircraft was in the vicinity of the Korean airliner on Aug. 31 when the airliner was initially detected by Soviet radar. Both aircraft were then in international airspace, and the U.S. aircraft never entered Soviet airspace. The U.S. routinely conducts unarmed RC-135 flights in international airspace off the Kamchatka Peninsula to monitor by technical means Soviet compliance with the SALT treaties. The Soviets conduct similar monitoring activities near U.S. missile-testing areas.

The Soviets are aware of our flights and track them routinely. They know that our aircraft do not enter their airspace. The Korean aircraft's inadvertent entry into Soviet territory should have been an early and strong indication to them that the flight was not a U.S. reconnaissance aircraft.

The Soviets traced the Korean aircraft and the U.S. aircraft separately and knew there were two aircraft in the area, so we do not think this was a case of mistaken identity. The closest point of approach was approximately 75 nautical miles while the U.S. aircraft was in its mission orbit. Later the U.S. aircraft crossed the path taken by the Korean airliner, but by then the airliner was almost 300 miles away. Still later, as the Korean airliner strayed off course and overflew Kamchatka Peninsula, it was initially identified by the Soviets as an RC-135 and then as an unidentified aircraft. Approximately two and a half hours after the U.S. and Korean aircraft were near each other in international space, the Soviets shot down the Korean airliner as it was exiting (or had exited) their territory west of Sakhalin Island, some 1,000 miles from the operating area of the U.S. aircraft.

During the two and one half hours of Soviet surveillance of the Korean aircraft, the Soviets had radar images (both ground and air) of the Korean 747. The two aircraft are distinctly different in shape and size. Their fighter aircraft also had visual contact with the Korean aircraft. The Su-15 and MiG-23 aircraft pilots whose voices are on the tape obtained by the U.S. and played for the congressional leadership never refer to the Korean aircraft as an RC-135, only as the "target." They made no serious effort to identify the aircraft or to warn it. They did not appear to care what it was. Instead, they were intent on killing it.

If the Soviets made a mistaken identification, which stretches the imagination, they have not said so to date. In fact, they have not to date admitted shooting down the Korean commercial aircraft with 269 people aboard. We continue to ask the Soviets for their full accounting of this incident.

The presence of a U.S. reconnaissance aircraft on a routine monitoring mission to assure Soviet compliance with the treaty obligation some 1,000 miles and two and a half hours' flight time from the scene of the shootdown in no way excuses or explains this act, which speaks for itself. In fact, the RC-135 in question, at the time KE 007 was shot down, had been on the ground at its home base in Alaska for more than one hour.

The United States had told the Soviets and the world in the clearest detailed terms that an RC-135 was involved. Pandora's Box had been opened.

To further confuse while amplifying, air force officers interviewed on the matter said that the RC-135 "would routinely have 'painted,' or registered with radar, the Korean plane as a matter of aerial safety. It could not be determined if the reconnaissance plane spotted Russian fighters on its radar."

They also said, "Air force planes on such missions rarely listen in on commercial airline radio frequencies. In addition, the reconnaissance planes' listening devices would be tuned to missile communications and not to air defense trans-missions. The technicians who operate listening and moni-toring devices rarely understand Russian. The technicians tape the information, then deliver it to intelligence analysts in Alaska to study."

The next day, Tuesday, September 6, with this choice new disclosure that the RC-135 was involved, the Soviet government issued a vituperative statement on the incident. At the end of its long discourse the claim was made that "the entire responsibility for this tragedy rests wholly and fully with the leaders of the United States of America."

The Soviet statement immediately seized upon the RC-135 disclosure, but at this date the alleged rendezvous had not yet been fabricated. However, the statement that one of the Soviet interceptors "controlled the actions of the American RC-135 plane" *had* been fabricated.

These are the two paragraphs that relate directly to the RC-135:

> The intruder plane entered the airspace over Kam-chatka in an area where a most important base of the strategic nuclear forces of the U.S.S.R. is located. At the same time – and this is now admitted by the American side – another spy plane of the United States Air Force, an RC-135 that is similar to it, was in the same area near the Soviet border on the same altitude.

Several Soviet interceptor planes were set aloft. One of them controlled the actions of the American RC-135 plane. A second flew into the area where the intruder plane was and signalled to it that it had intruded into the airspace of the U.S.S.R. The warnings were ignored.

The KAL 747 is now a spy plane "with another spy plane." How a Soviet interceptor controlled the actions of the RC-135 has never been explained or, for that matter, referred to by the Soviets in any subsequent statements.

The stage now moves to Moscow and a "spellbinding performance" – according to the *New York Times* – by Marshal Nikolai V. Ogarkov, Chief of the General Staff of the Soviet Armed Forces and First Deputy Minister of Defense.

He would preside at the first-ever press conference with western world media conducted by a Soviet official of his high rank. There was simply no precedent for this action in the U.S.S.R. – a country where foreigners are prohibited from even taking a picture of a man in uniform and which has the most formidable secrecy barrier of any nation in the world. It was astonishing to the press that the Politburo would be sufficiently moved by its world image problems to produce the top soldier in the Soviet Union to face what would be two hours of intensive and often embarrassingly direct questioning by foreign reporters.

The fact that Andropov and his colleagues would direct or authorize Ogarkov's appearance before the world's television, radio and print journalists, taking the chance that their senior soldier might say the wrong thing, was testimony not only to their confidence in him but also to the depth of their concern about how the act was publicly perceived outside the Soviet Union. The press conference was also a clever use (perhaps manipulation is a better word) by the Soviets of the power of the press of the western world. The press would carry to a watching, listening and reading audience of hundreds of millions of people a carefully orchestrated propaganda message delivered by the Soviets' top military man, a person with the substantial credibility of his high rank and, as the two-hour session proved, enormous presence and panache.

But was that the real reason for putting Ogarkov front and center? Or was the press conference also designed to obscure the question of who in the Soviet hierarchy had given the order to shoot Flight 007 down? This question will be considered in more detail at a later stage.

The press conference produced one major bombshell. It was the carefully orchestrated and developed scenario – produced over the previous four days by ingenious Soviet propagandists – of the role played by the American RC-135.

Much of the propaganda information published by the Soviet Union for foreign consumption is called "disinformation." The publication on September 4 and 5, 1983, by the Reagan Administration of the "role" of the RC-135 can be called not "disinformation" but "dumbinformation." As they say in the United States, it's "shooting yourself in the foot."

As the enormously impressed *New York Times* put it on Saturday, September 10:

> Nikolai V. Ogarkov, the large gold stars of a Marshal on his shoulder boards and the medal of a Hero of the Soviet Union surmounting nine rows of campaign ribbons, held the jampacked conference hall spellbound as he reconstructed in slow succinct cadences the Soviet government's case that Korean Air Lines Flight 007 had been on a "deliberate, thoroughly planned intelligence mission" when an Su-15 jet fighter brought it down with an air-to-air missile.
>
> At one point the rugged 65-year-old Marshal wielded a long pointer to trace the flight's last two and a half hours on a giant wall map marked with the normal air corridor across the North Pacific . . .

Wielding his pointer, Ogarkov traced, on the huge wall chart that had been prepared for his momentous press show, oval circles around the 747's track just before it had first crossed into Soviet territory northeast of Kamchatka.

This was the Marshal's bombshell. This revelation had been invented and developed by his staff in the five days since President Reagan's fortuitous September 4 disclosure that an RC-135 was in the area.

Using the full credibility of his rank, Marshal Ogarkov would now appear on television sets around the world with the incriminating revelation that the RC-135 actually rendezvoused with the 747, thereby well and truly "proving" that the Korean jumbo jet was a villainous spy plane.

Standing at the wall chart, the tip of his pointer confidently tracing the paths of the two aircraft drawn on the map in heavy black lines, he said:

> Let me turn your particular attention to the fact that departure of the plane – the entry of the plane into the zone controlled by the Russian Air Defense Forces – occurs specifically at the point at which . . . American RC-135 planes regularly operate. And on that very flight route RC-135 was found by the Soviet forces on September 1, [with] the Soviet radio-electronics surveillance devices. The plane operated in that area for about two hours.
>
> At 4 p.m. exactly in the same area approximately like the other, drew up at 8,000 meters, another airplane was detected. At 5, those two planes rendezvoused and for some time, approximately for 10 minutes in that region, they were flying side by side. Then one of them could be observed, followed by the radios, turned back and flew to Alaska while the second plane went straight to Petropavlovsk in Kamchatka.
>
> This led the American-Soviet control points to the result that an American airplane was entering the Russian airspace. Let me ask the question: What was the point . . . of that entry? Obviously, the flight of this plane was being controlled – precisely controlled, I would state. And it was deliberate – that entry was deliberate.

During the long question period that followed his opening statement, Marshal Ogarkov reiterated the new rendezvous claim, which, for the Russians, proved that the United States Air Force "obviously played the control" of the Korean 747 in the initial phase of its entry into Soviet airspace.

In propaganda terms the rendezvous claim was highly successful in convincing people all over the world, and particularly in the United States, that the Korean airliner had in fact been on an electronic espionage mission across Kamchatka and Sakhalin Island for and on behalf of the United States of America.

The declared objective of the Soviet Union was to shift the blame for the destruction of the 747 and the murder of its 269 occupants on to the shoulders of the United States. Thanks to the gratuitous admission of the Reagan Administration that a USAF RC-135 had been in the area of the 747, the inventive Soviets were able to fabricate a convincing and credible rendezvous story that enabled them to achieve this goal. Millions of people in the western world now believe that the two aircraft did in fact rendezvous, that the 747 was on an electronic espionage mission controlled by the United States, that the Soviets were therefore justified in shooting the aircraft down and that the United States is responsible for the tragedy.

This is one of the most successful propaganda achievements in modern times. As the Reagan Administration has learned, the Russians are excellent in the field of propaganda and disinformation. They are particularly adept because the truth means nothing to them. They have no hesitation in lying, as the RC-135/KAL 747 rendezvous story clearly demonstrates. That rendezvous never happened.

The rueful reaction of Senator Byrd after the White House briefing on Sunday, September 4, should now be echoed by all the members of the Reagan Administration who had a hand in the decision to go public about the presence of the RC-135. To repeat the words of Senator Byrd, "I'm sorry it was even mentioned." The President had done a superb job of shooting himself in the foot.

9

OTHER SOVIET AIR ATTACKS

ANY PILOT WHO flies the R20 route from Anchorage to Seoul knows that he runs the risk of being shot down by the Soviets if he goes off course and, for whatever reason, enters Soviet airspace.

There is little doubt that Captain Chun knew of the Soviet propensity for shooting.

Assuming that he did, then if he deliberately set course direct from Anchorage to Seoul intending to overfly Kamchatka and Sakhalin, he must have believed the Soviet Air Defense Forces fighters as directed by the ADF's ground radar units would not be able to catch him; or, if they did find him, that they would identify the aircraft, see that it was a commercial passenger jet and not shoot it down. Either the Soviet interceptors would escort the 747 out of their airspace or they would force it to land at one of their bases.

Probably the Korean captain believed that, notwithstanding the 1978 shooting down of a KAL 707, no human being, even a Soviet fighter pilot, would deliberately push a firing button that would launch rockets or fire cannon to kill a planeload of two or three hundred people.

Since 1950 there have been twenty-seven incidents of Soviet fighter aircraft shooting at planes that had intruded into their airspace.

All of these attacks except three were against military aircraft, almost all of them American.

The three exceptions were: a Soviet attack on a French airliner on April 29, 1952, in which two passengers were injured; a June 3, 1954, attack on a Belgian transport carrying livestock, in Yugoslav airspace, in which one crew member was killed and two were injured; and an April 20, 1978, attack on a South Korean airliner that inadvertently crossed into Soviet territory en route to Seoul from Paris, in which two passengers were killed and thirteen hurt.

Captain Chun was certainly aware of the incident in which a fellow Korean captain, Kim Chang Kyu, flying a KAL Boeing 707 on a scheduled Paris-to-Seoul flight went astray on a course that should have taken him over the top of the Earth near the North Pole, then down into Korea just outside of Soviet airspace.

Like Flight 007 it was a nighttime flight. The aircraft was not fitted with the later Inertial Navigation Systems and so had on board a navigator equipped with a sextant and gyroscopic compass. The navigator would have to use his instruments frequently when transiting the polar regions in the dark. There would be no landmarks visible and no radio beacons readily available against which to check his position. The navigator became hopelessly lost and the aircraft flew well off course and into Soviet airspace.

In the early light of dawn that morning, a Soviet fighter appeared off to the right of the 707. The co-pilot saw it and the red Soviet star on the aircraft's tail, but Captain Kim did not get a good look at it because the aircraft appeared only once. International interception rules, on the other hand, require intercepting fighters to come up on the left side of the intercepted airplane where the captain sits.

Kim did what he was supposed to do. He reduced his speed and turned his landing lights off and on repeatedly to indicate to the interceptor that he was prepared to follow directions. He also tried to establish radio contact, but that was not possible because the two aircraft did not have a common frequency.

The fighter fell back behind the KAL 707, took aim and fired a rocket that hit the left wing of the aircraft – fortunately well out from the fuselage – shearing off almost fifteen feet of the aircraft's 131-foot wingspan. Shrapnel ripped a hole in the front of the fuselage, killing two passengers and injuring

The Su-15 interceptor pilot 805.

The U.S.S.R.'s Sukhoi Su-15 interceptor.

RC-135:
Wing span: 145 ft. 9 in.
Length overall: 152 ft. 11 in.
Length of fuselage: 145 ft. 6 in.
Height overall: 42 ft. 5 in.

Boeing 747-200
Wing span: 195 ft. 8 in.
Length overall: 231 ft. 4 in.
Length of fuselage: 225 ft. 2 in.
Height overall: 63 ft. 5 in.

The RC-135 (top) and the Boeing 747-200.

Captain Chun of Flight 007.

Blasted piece of Flight 007's tailfin.

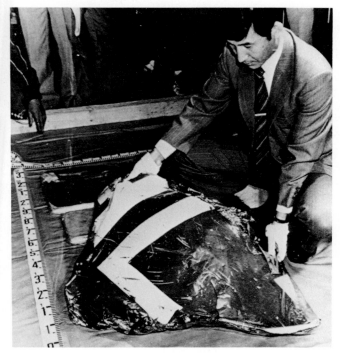

Cockpit of the Boeing 747.

○ INERTIAL NAVIGATION SYSTEMS

▭ AUTOPILOT PANEL HEADING (HDG) SELECTOR SWITCH

▫ WEATHER RADAR

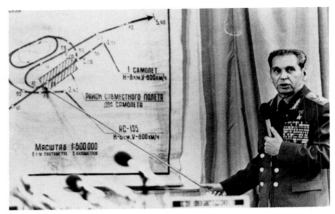

Marshal Ogarkov and the RC-135/Flight 007 rendezvous map, September 9, 1983.

The crucial U.N. Security Council vote on September
13. Ambassadors Sir John Thomson of the U.K. and
Jeane Kirkpatrick of the U.S. vote for the motion while

U.S.S.R. Ambassador Oleg Troyanovsky waits to vote against.

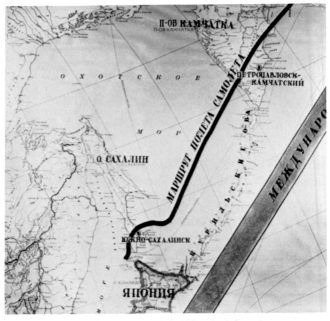

The Flight 007 track claimed by Marshal Ogarkov at
the September 9 press conference.

several others. There was instant decompression, forcing the captain to dive his aircraft down to 3,000 feet from his cruising altitude of 35,000. The high-altitude, killing cold and lack of oxygen had to be avoided immediately.

Eventually, Captain Kim found a frozen lake that he could safely land on. He did a wheels-up landing on the lake near the town of Kem, south of Murmansk. The Soviets made the same claims about Kim and his 707 that they did about Flight 007. They said they had tracked him for more than two hours, had flown around the plane and had fired tracers in front of the aircraft.

Captain Kim was later cleared of any fault by Korean Air Lines and the South Korean government authorities and reinstated as a captain. Today he is a 747 veteran, often flying the Anchorage-Seoul route.

He is one Korean Air Lines captain who would never consider taking a 747 into Soviet airspace no matter what the reason. He is also a captain who uses his weather radar in the mapping mode whenever he is flying the R20 route from Anchorage to Seoul. He likes to know exactly where those Kuril Islands are on his right, and he never wants to see the coast of the Kamchatka Peninsula appear on his weather radar screen.

10

THE ROCKETS' IMPACT
ON FLIGHT 007

WHAT HAPPENED to the KAL 747 and the people in it when
the two ANAB missiles slammed into it can be assessed
by considering several factors: the location of the wreckage;
the type of debris found; the length of time it took the main
remnant of the aircraft to reach the sea; and, of course, the
missiles themselves.

The two ANAB rockets were slung under the wings of the
aircraft. The wingspan of the Su-15 was about thirty-one
feet. Each of the missiles was on a pylon about three feet
inboard from the wing tip. Thus, the distance between the
two rockets was approximately twenty-four feet. This is an
important factor when considering where each of the rockets
impacted the 747.

As has already been mentioned, one of the rockets was
infra-red heat-seeking, which means that it would follow one
of the four rivers of heat being thrown out by each of the huge
turbo-jet engines slung underneath the wings of the 747. The
747's inboard engines, both port and starboard, are approximately thirty feet out from the fuselage. The outboard
engines are another thirty feet beyond those.

The other rocket was radar homing, which means it would
lock on to the largest part of the aircraft seen from the rear
and perhaps slightly to the side. The rocket's target therefore
would be the huge circular fuselage. The tail would be the
point of impact. Indeed the Su-15 pilot, 805, would have his
aircraft's radar as well as his radar-directed rocket "locked
on" to the 747's fuselage.

As the seventy pound high-explosive warhead of the radar homing missile hit the 747, it would have penetrated the tail section for some distance even as it was detonating. At the same time, the heat-seeking rocket that was launched twenty-four feet away from it on a parallel course would have smashed right into the inboard engine on the port or starboard side of the 747. If the infra-red heat-seeking rocket had been mounted under the right wing of the Su-15, it is likely that it would have hit the right inboard engine; or, if the position of the rockets on the Su-15 had been reversed, the left inboard engine.

On September 9, a piece of the metal tail of the Boeing 747 was found on a beach on the island of Hokkaido near Wakkanai. (That is, coincidentally, the location of the Japanese military radar station whose operators had watched the 747 fall from 35,000 feet into the Sea of Japan, believing that it was a Soviet transport.) The piece of the tail found was white with the letter "L" on a red background and what resembled part of a letter "H" and the number seven. The KAL 747 had its number, HL7442, painted on its tail in white lettering on a red field (see photo section).

The piece of the vertical section of the plane's huge fin measured just 32 inches by 28 inches. The only way it could have been cut out of the huge fin itself would be by a massive explosion centered near that piece of the tail. The towering tail would have been blown into many pieces.

If the tail had not been hit and had remained attached to the fuselage as the aircraft descended into the sea, that strongly constructed section would not have disintegrated on impact in such a way as to produce small pieces. Such a result could only have been caused by an explosion.

That same explosion from the radar-directed missile, which would have been travelling at over 2,000 miles per hour, would have penetrated the aluminum skin of the tail section and gone straight into the rear of the fuselage, instantly killing everyone in the aircraft and showering them with shards of glass and metal. The only people who might have survived that blast momentarily were the captain, co-pilot and flight engineer, who remained alive just long enough (fifty-eight seconds) to blurt out to Narita control: "KAL 007 all engines . . . rapid decompression . . . one zero one . . . two delta . . . ." The first part meant that all engines had failed and that cabin pressure was going. What the "one zero one" and "two delta" meant is not known.

The other missile, impacting up the tail pipe of an inboard engine, would destroy it, instantly shattering the engine's blades into thousands of lethal pieces and opening up the side of the fuselage like a tin can as the force of the explosion and attendant fire ripped off the wing, spewing thousands of gallons of jet fuel into the short-lived inferno.

Which rocket hit first can be determined by examining their respective ranges. The one with the higher range would have hit sooner because it would have had to develop a higher speed to achieve the longer distance. It is therefore likely that the first missile to impact, assuming both bursts were fired simultaneously, would be the radar-controlled rocket. It would sever the electrical systems, shutting down engine instruments and causing the pilot to say, "all engines." Concurrently, the heat-seeking rocket would be slamming into one of the inboard engines, severing the wing. The two impacts would be almost simultaneous. From the time 805 reported that he had launched to the time he reported the target destroyed was only two seconds.

Thirty-five thousand feet below, on the black rolling surface of the Sea of Japan near the island of Sakhalin, Japanese squid fishermen on two boats saw the sky brighten high above them with a flash like a comet, and heard the deep thundering sound of two explosions.

Flight 007 and all the people on board had been killed.

The severed wing and pieces from it began to flutter down, spinning and turning.

Pieces of the shattered tail spread out in the night air like snowflakes making their way aimlessly downward. The flaming fuselage, in a ball of fire generated by the explosives combined with the fuel, continued straight on for a few moments. Bits of bodies and clothes and paraphernalia untouched by the fire were blasted out the back by the force of the initial explosion. Then, with the engines silent and the flames rapidly dying out, the powerless, one-winged carcass began to roll slowly over and over like a huge game bird struck dead in mid-air by a hunter's shotgun. Twisting and turning, it arced down toward the sea leaving a trail of mid-air flotsam and jetsam. It was only those things that would float on the water, the flotsam and jetsam, that would be recovered from the wide area of the Sea of Japan west of Sakhalin. The main remnants hit the surface of the water then disappeared silently into it.

According to the Soviets, debris was later found in four separate areas north of Moneron Island off the west coast of Sakhalin (See Map 10:1). It is likely that the main fuselage section was immediately to the west of Moneron, that the wing was closest to the Siberian coast, that the pieces of the tail section were to the northeast, close to the Sakhalin coastline, and that a shower of lighter material was carried and widely scattered by the wind. (Only moments before it was

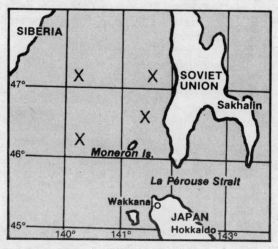

Map 10:1   X marks the location of the KE 007 debris.

destroyed, at 18:26 GMT, Flight 007 reported the wind to be a strong 45 knots.)

On September 9, a child's body embedded with splinters of metal and glass was pulled from the waters northwest of Hokkaido. On a beach near Wakkanai, other parts of the wreckage had been found: metal fragments, an oxygen mask, a piece of heat insulating material and a cushion with both Korean characters and English letters printed on it.

By the time the search for debris and, in particular, the black boxes was finished in early November (neither of the black boxes was discovered), only five bodies, or pieces of them, had been recovered. All had fragments of metal and glass in them. Their dismembered state was evidence that they had been through an explosion, although there was no indication of fire. Those people were probably sitting close to the rear of the aircraft and were blown out by the initial explosion before the fire touched them.

Pieces of the wing flaps and ailerons, sections of cabin seats, paper cups, vinyl bags, aluminum honeycomb material, calling cards of Chang Ma Son, a Taiwanese passenger, an identification card of a Canadian, Mary Jane Hendrie, running shoes, trousers and other pieces of clothing – in all, some one thousand pieces of material from the aircraft – were collected. This included the seventy-six objects in five crates that the Soviets turned over to a party of Japanese and U.S. government officials and U.S. naval personnel on Sakhalin Island on September 26.

There were reports that, from the moment the missiles hit, it took some twelve minutes for the ravaged fuselage and its remaining wing to strike the surface of the Sea of Japan. Unidentified military officials were purported to have said on September 12 that the aircraft had fallen in "vast spirals" until it reached 2,000 feet, and then plunged vertically into the water, twelve minutes after the attack.

Given the nature of the explosion in the tail and the fact that a wing was shed, it is difficult, from an aerodynamic point of view, to believe that the remaining bulk of the machine could have "spiralled." Rather, without one wing and the tail, it would probably have rolled or tumbled. Either way, it would have rapidly decelerated from its over 500-mile-an-hour cruising speed as it fell in an arc. If we remember that the 747 was flying at about six miles above the surface of the sea when it was hit and roughly triple that height giving a distance travelled to the sea surface of eighteen miles, then the average fall speed is 360 miles an hour or six miles a minute. The best probability is that it would have taken three minutes for the main body of the aircraft to hit the surface. On the other hand, the fluttering aerodynamic wing falling through the night air like a leaf and presenting a substantial radar image might well have taken longer.

According to retired Japanese Air Force General Goro Takeda, a former chairman of Japan's Joint Chiefs of Staff, the Japanese military radar monitors were correct when they reported that the jetliner crashed into the sea only three minutes after the Soviet pilot said, "The target is destroyed." That estimate is much more realistic than the eventual twelve-minute figure, given the speed at which the airplane was flying when it was hit and the relatively short distance to the sea, with an arc of perhaps eight miles to travel. In a statement made in Tokyo on September 14, Takeda noted that Japan's Self-Defense Forces insisted that the jet crashed into the sea near Moneron Island at 3:29 a.m. Japanese time (18:29 GMT) three minutes after it was hit. As General Takeda pointed out, if the plane had flown an additional nine minutes, it would have crashed more than seventy kilometers (forty-five miles) away from the spot the Japanese radar had pinpointed, and where the Soviet search activity was going on. To Takeda's statement, it must be added that the aircraft could not have flown another forty-five miles with one wing and the tail missing. Nor could it have been in the long spiral invented by those trying to sort out why it had taken twelve minutes from the time of destruction to crash into the sea.

How long it took for the instant wreckage created by the deadly ANAB missiles to reach the surface is, in the end, of no importance. What is significant, however, is that the efficient ANABs did their work quickly. The innocent souls on board did not have to suffer through a twelve-minute – or even three-minute – ride in a living hell. Mercifully, their lives were snuffed out in the twinkling of an eye, a fact for which their bereaved families and loved ones and friends can be grateful.

BOOK TWO

THE AFTERMATH

11

JAPAN, THE TAPES AND THE SEARCH FOR THE BLACK BOXES

THE AFTERMATH of the event – the killing of Flight 007 in mid-air – began with the Japanese military operators at Wakkanai watching what they thought was a big Soviet transport aircraft escorted by four fighters suddenly leave its altitude of about 35,000 feet and, within three minutes, disappear completely off the scope. There could be only one interpretation. The transport aircraft had crashed into the Sea of Japan.

It was Thursday, the first day of September. The Boeing 747 had been destroyed in the moonlit darkness at 18:26 GMT, 3:26 a.m. Japanese local time.

The Japanese military radar operators knew that they had witnessed the crash of a large transport aircraft, but they had no reason to believe that it was anything other than a Soviet machine. Even so it was a startling event for them to watch, which they probably did with a certain detachment, since whatever crew might have been in the plane were represented only by a blip on their screens.

Because they believed it was a Russian transport they had seen, the crash was no concern of theirs or of the Japanese Defense Agency (JDA). The Soviets would look after the situation themselves. At the same time there was no need to alert the Japanese air traffic control center at Narita. Even if it had been alerted, the controllers there would have been certain that all the civilian airliners in their control area had been accounted for and were on their flight-planned routes.

They certainly would have no record of a 747 over Sakhalin Island. That would be utter madness.

However, at Narita they had received, at 3:27 a.m., the "start of an unintelligible transmission" from Flight 007.

Later the Japanese Ministry of Foreign Affairs made public a transcript of radio communications between Flight 007 and Narita, saying:

> Narita fully expected to receive the pilot's report that he had passed Nokka [another way-point] 270 km [168 mi.] east southeast of Kushiro at 3:26 a.m. It was not until 3:27 a.m. that there was any suspicion that there might be trouble [e.g., radio failure] with Korean Air Lines Flight 007 near Nokka.

The ministry stated that for approximately seventeen minutes, from 3:12 to 3:29 a.m. (which was the correct time the 747 hit the sea, not 3:38), the Air Self-Defense Force radar station at Wakkanai sighted and recorded an aircraft flying southwest over Sakhalin Island approximately one hundred miles north of Wakkanai. The statement went on: "But there was no way that the Air Self-Defense Force could have known at that time that this aircraft was Korean Air Lines Flight 007."

The Air Self-Defense Force was not attempting to follow Flight 007 on route R20 because it did not follow the civilian airliners on their normal commercial routes. The Air Self-Defense Force was interested in just that, defense, and against the Soviets. It was Soviet airspace that the force surveyed and monitored at all times. However, the military radar "rather suddenly picked up that aircraft on their radar at 3:12 a.m. when it entered the airspace over Sakhalin, and even then it was sighted as an unidentified aircraft."

The ministry hastened to add, and justifiably so, that "Japan was in no position to warn Korean Air Lines Flight 007, since we had no way of knowing that the aircraft had strayed from its route."

The expected mandatory waypoint report for passage at

Nokka did not come. Just that garbled, final transmission (a recording of which was later enhanced and found to be the report that Flight 007 had lost all engines and was suffering rapid decompression). There was, of course, no report from 007 at Noho, 163 miles southwest of Nokka.

Narita air traffic control could not raise the KAL 747. Perhaps it had lost all its radios. It couldn't have crashed. After all it was a 747.

The jumbo jet's estimated arrival time at Seoul was 5:53 a.m. local Korean time. By the time the 747 was scheduled to report in to the Seoul air controllers, Seoul was aware that there had been no transmissions to Japanese air controllers since the garbled Nokka one. The Seoul operators were watching for the aircraft on their radar screens, but it never appeared.

At that point the alarm went. Flight 007 was well and truly missing.

The checking and cross-checking now began in earnest, with queries going from the Narita air traffic control network to the Japan Defense Agency. In turn, a signal went out saying that Korean Air Lines Flight 007, a Boeing 747, was missing on a flight from Anchorage to Seoul via Route R20. Details of all recorded radio transmissions were also communicated and the double-checking process began.

It was at Wakkanai that all the pieces fitted together. The radar operators confirmed that they had sighted and recorded an aircraft flying southwest over Sakhalin approximately one hundred miles north of Wakkanai, and had watched it crash. But there was no way they could have known it was Flight 007. The next step was to check with the Japan Defense Agency and for any Soviet radio communications that might have been intercepted by the Rescue Co-ordination Center of the Japanese Ministry of Transport. The center had a voice-activated recording machine going at all times, monitoring every communications frequency used by the Soviets in controlling their fighters. The Rescue Co-ordination people ran the tapes back to the relevant time period. They could hear certain key Russian words such as "missile" and "shoot down." It was then a matter of getting the Soviet radio traffic translated.

As that slow process was going on, officials in South Korea, Japan and the United States were scrambling to find out what had happened to the overdue aircraft.

Finally, some seven and a half hours after Flight 007 had last been heard from, the South Korean Foreign Ministry decided that it had to make a statement using the best information it had to that point. The ministry said it had received U.S. intelligence reports that the aircraft "had not exploded, or crashed, but was known to have been forced to land at Sakhalin." A Korean Air Lines representative said that the aircraft had landed safely on the island.

The message to the world was that everything was all right, the passengers were safe and details would follow. As usual it would be difficult to deal with the Soviets.

In Japan the Air Self-Defense Force claimed that its radar had not picked up an aircraft at the location given by the pilot of Flight 007 in his last radio contact. The radar operators at Wakkanai had recorded an unidentified plane over Sakhalin at about the same time.

The Japanese Maritime Safety Agency was in the process of making radio contact and inquiries with more than one hundred of that country's fishing boats operating in the Sea of Japan to the west of Sakhalin, the area where the Japanese radar had seen an aircraft go down. In addition, eight patrol boats and four aircraft were dispatched to conduct a search.

What is clear in retrospect is that, while the South Korean government was convinced – or was it wishful thinking? – that the KAL 747 had landed safely (under compulsion or otherwise) on Sakhalin Island, the Japanese were acting on the information they had from their own military radar. An aircraft had gone down in the Sea of Japan just to the west of Sakhalin Island. It could well be the 747. If there was any chance that it was (and all the preliminary information pointed to it being the 747) Japan would get rescue vessels there as quickly as possible, just in case.

Furthermore, the Japanese Maritime Safety Agency had been given permission to send two patrol boats and a helicopter into Soviet territorial waters to conduct a search there.

Meanwhile, in Tokyo, a spokesman for the Soviet embassy quite prudently said, when asked, that he had no information on the fate of Flight 007. It would not be long until he had more information than he would want to know about.

The propaganda and counter-propaganda game was about to begin. It would be the major element of the aftermath, as the United States and the Soviet Union sought to win the "hearts and minds" of the world's public.

By the late afternoon of Thursday, September 1, the translation of the tapes of the Soviet fighter pilot's communications with ground control had been completed, checked and double-checked. The cautious Japanese were appalled by what they had on their hands. Would they give the transcript to the United States, now their great ally, their major marketplace and the principal defender of Japan's sovereignty against the growing threat of the Soviet Union in the Kuril-Sakhalin-Kamchatka area? There was no doubt about the decision. The transcript of the tape was immediately transmitted electronically to the U.S. Secretary of State, George Shultz, in Washington.

Meanwhile the Japanese government had to decide how it would handle the public disclosure of this explosive information. The decision was to hold an emergency press conference.

This was called for 8:20 p.m. in Tokyo.

In Moscow, before the tapes had been translated, Mr. Hasashi Owada of the Japanese Embassy had acted on the instructions of his government and had been in frequent telephone contact with the Soviet Foreign Ministry, repeatedly asking about the Soviet Union's knowledge of how the plane had disappeared. At 7:00 a.m. Moscow time, he was finally told by a Foreign Ministry duty officer that the 747 was not on Sakhalin.

In another telephone conversation four and a half hours later, a Soviet Foreign Ministry official confirmed that the plane had not "landed" in the Soviet Union, saying that it was not in Soviet territory at all. By the time Mr. Owada had received this information and passed it back to Tokyo, his government knew what had happened to Flight 007. It had been shot down by the Soviets.

Even so, when Foreign Minister Shintaro Abe appeared at the emergency press conference at 8:20 p.m., he said only that, on the basis of information his government had received, it "appears likely" that the Russians had shot down the 747.

He was reluctant to say more because there was an understanding with Secretary Shultz in Washington that the U.S. government would handle the breaking of the news. Both Japan and the United States had lost a comparable number of nationals in the disaster. But it was the United States that was the superpower, and that had close relations with the South Koreans, who have held Japan at arm's length since World War II. And it was the United States that had so much electronic and other surveillance equipment as well as other military installations to protect near the Kuril-Kamchatka-Sakhalin area.

There was another interesting disclosure in Tokyo on September 1. It was revealed that the Japanese had monitored conversations between the Soviet ground control and the fighter that had fired at the KAL 747.

This is of interest because of the subsequent furor over the question of whether tapes had in fact been made of conversations between ground control and the pilots. The existence of such tapes was later denied, both by Japan and by the United States. If the ground control voices had indeed been recorded on the so-called second tape, many still-open questions would have been answered.

These were the key orders and responses purportedly recorded about 3:20 a.m. Japanese time between the Soviet ground control, Deputat, and the fighter plane:

"Take aim at the target."
"Aim taken."

"Fire."

"Fired."

According to undisclosed military sources, three such sets of communications were monitored. Apparently this was done by the military who, with their facilities at Wakkanai and elsewhere, could reasonably have been expected to have set up a system for monitoring not only transmissions from Soviet pilots to the ground, but ground-to-air instructions as well. In addition to the three two-way conversations between the ground and the aircraft, the Japanese facilities also monitored Soviet orders in dispatching eight ships to the area in the Sea of Japan near Moneron Island, thirty nautical miles off the southwestern Sakhalin coast, where the 747 had probably gone down.

At his press conference, Foreign Minister Shintaro Abe also said that he was appointing a task force to liaise with the U.S., the Soviet Union and South Korea in order to find out what actually led to the shooting down of the Korean aircraft.

As the first day of September 1983 passed into history, officials at the White House and at the State Department in Washington and in the Kremlin, at the offices of TASS and at military headquarters in Moscow were working feverishly to analyse the reports that flooded in as the situation unfolded. Not surprisingly, the Washington story would be quite different from the Moscow story. The volume, pitch and tone of the upcoming screaming and roaring match between the American Eagle and the Russian Bear would be as intense, uncompromising and filled with mendacity and mordancy as any confrontation the two had had in recent times.

Caught in between the two superpower antagonists, the Japanese kept a low profile.

In Washington, Secretary Shultz was ready to tell the story – so far as it was known – of what had happened. At an emotional press conference, but without referring to the existence of tapes or any of the sources of his intelligence, he gave a description of the event that shook the journalists with its particularity and specificity.

On Thursday morning, after reviewing the transcript of the

Soviet fighter pilot's taped reports, along with other information that was coming in, Shultz was convinced that the Soviets were guilty. He immediately decided to go public with his accusatory statement and did so as soon as it was prepared. In it he urgently demanded an explanation from the Soviet Union, saying "the United States reacts with revulsion to this attack. The loss of life appears to be heavy. We can see no excuse whatsoever for this appalling act." The Soviet government launched its first return salvo a few hours later, accusing the American authorities of resorting to "all kinds of dirty insinuations about the U.S.S.R." and claiming that the statement of President Reagan which followed that of Secretary Shultz was "impudent" and "slanderous."

The war of words was on.

Early in the morning of Friday, September 2, Japanese Foreign Minister Abe did what he was to do several times in the next few days. He summoned the Soviet Ambassador to Japan, Vladimir Y. Pavlov. The time was 3:50 a.m., a little more than twenty-four hours after the destruction of the 747. The Soviets had made no admissions about shooting down the aircraft. In fact, a government statement was being prepared in Moscow, to be issued through TASS that day, which in effect would say that they had not shot it down.

Pavlov was reported to have said that traces of an aircraft crash had been found near Moneron Island, but he would not admit that these traces had anything to do with Flight 007.

Later that day, the Japanese Broadcasting Corporation said that tape recordings had been made of both sides of the conversation between Soviet ground stations and the interceptors they were controlling. The tapes supposedly covered the full two and a half hours during which the Korean aircraft was being tracked by Soviet radar and the Soviet fighters were trying to intercept it. These were the so-called second tapes, with their military origins. However, the only tape that was made public was the one of 805's air-to-ground reports recorded by the Maritime Safety Agency of the Japanese Ministry of Transport.

On September 2, the first piece of hard evidence surfaced to prove that something had indeed happened over Sakhalin Island in the early morning hours of September 1. As *Newsweek* later reported, at the moment the missiles struck the 747 a Japanese fishing boat, *Chidoru Maru*, was netting squid twenty-four miles northwest of Russia's Moneron Island. The skipper, Shizuka Hayashi, and his six crew members heard approaching jets. Then "a violent explosion shook the air and a brilliant orange flash lit the southeastern sky. The light flared for several seconds, succeeded by a round of fireworks and another less-powerful explosion. After five or six minutes, the smell of burning fuel wafted over the boat."

The pieces were now fitting together. Not only had Hayashi and his crew witnessed the explosion, but also they had heard not just one jet aircraft approaching, but "jets."

Following the lead of President Reagan and Secretary Shultz in the United States, the Japanese government made a condemning statement on September 2. Following a meeting of the Japanese Cabinet, a press conference in Tokyo was told by Chief Cabinet Secretary Masaharu Gotoda that the Soviet action against a civilian aircraft was "unforgivable" in any sense. Referring to the Japanese nationals on board the aircraft, Gotoda said that the Japanese government demanded an immediate, frank and sincere response from the Soviet Union.

On Saturday, September 3, the Japanese government appeared to be staying with its policy of keeping a low profile and letting the superpowers have at each other.

The Japanese Broadcasting Corporation was saying that it had evidence that the order to fire on the South Korean plane had come from a ground-control station. The corporation had broadcast a message, reportedly radioed by the Russian pilot, that said: "It is now within sight. The plane is not yet aware of us" (this was close to what the later released tapes indicated), "missile fired" and "shot down." The Japanese government refused to say whether any recordings of the conversations existed at all. Furthermore Foreign Ministry officials refused to comment on the Japanese Broadcasting

Corporation's statement that the government would be prepared to make the tapes public if it was unhappy with the Soviet handling of the crisis. No comment.

During the Soviet Ambassador's command visit to the Japanese Foreign Ministry that day (it was the third time since the event), and in his first meeting with the Foreign Minister, Mr. Abe, Ambassador Pavlov was told that Japan was concerned about Moscow's refusal to give them any details and about its refusal to allow Japanese searching vessels into Soviet territorial weaters. Relations with the Soviets had become increasingly strained even before the 747 incident. The Japanese had expressed concern about the Soviet deployment of MiG-23 fighters on Sakhalin Island right on the very doorstep of Japan. The Russians had replied that they had done so because U.S. F-16 fighters had been moved into the air base at Misawa. In addition, the Japanese were most unhappy that the Soviets had moved some thirty aircraft to the disputed island of Etorofu at the southern tip of the Kuril chain just to the north of Hokkaido, and had stationed troops and carried out military exercises there.

At the meeting with Mr. Abe, Ambassador Pavlov, true to Soviet form, attempted to turn the tables by complaining that the Japanese government and media were attempting to stir up anti-Soviet feelings. Pavlov knew the extent of those feelings because of loud demonstrations put on by upwards of 2,000 people protesting outside his own embassy in Tokyo's Kamiyacho district. The embassy was ringed with people and sound trucks shouting anti-Soviet statements.

Meanwhile the search went on in the Sea of Japan.

Japanese boats in the area near Moneron Island had found nothing substantial, but on Saturday, September 3, a patrol boat of the Japanese Maritime Safety Agency had found some floating insulation material. Tests were to be done to see if it had come from the 747. At a location eighteen miles north of Moneron Island, some plastic bags with Korean writing on them were found.

The intensive search went on, with American craft arriving on the scene. The Soviet flotilla was already there. The prizes that all were after by this time were the black boxes – either the CVR, the cockpit voice recorder, or the DFDR, the Digital Flight Data Recorder, or, ideally, both. If the searchers could find one they could probably find the other, because both had been installed in the tail section of the 747.

On September 5, there was talk that Japan might reveal the military, as opposed to the civilian, intelligence it had gathered on the 747 destruction. The information was believed to include, once again, the taped communications between Soviet ground control and the interceptor aircraft. What would be new would be the Japanese Defense Agency radar-scan record of the airliner during the seventeen minutes that it was on the Wakkanai radar.

In a press conference, the Japanese Defense Minister, Tazuo Tanikawa, said that his Defense Agency would decide whether to make public the tape it had given to Washington.

He was referring to the tape that President Reagan had used, in translation, to brief Congressional leaders and others at the White House on Sunday. However, Reagan Administration officials had already said that that tape would be made public.

Up until then, the Soviet Union had continued to deny requests that Japanese search ships be allowed inside its territorial limits. Nevertheless the United States and Japan intended to make a joint application to the Soviets to allow both Japan and the United States to search in Soviet waters.

Even though the U.S.S.R. was a member of the International Civil Aviation Organization (ICAO) and a signatory to the treaty organizing it, the Soviets had not recognized a provision in the treaty which would allow search and rescue operations for foreign aircraft or ships to enter its waters. The Soviets were not completely rigid on this point, because in the first few hours after the event, Soviet authorities had given permission for a helicopter and two patrol boats to search in territorial waters. It was undoubtedly the later intervention of the Americans with their sophisticated small submarines and other underwater gear that brought the

Soviet negative. Letting in the Japanese to do the underwater search for the black boxes was one thing, but letting in the Americans with their undersea technology and retrieval skills was quite another. The answer was "nyet."

Outside Soviet waters, in the international section of the Sea of Japan, some fourteen Japanese Coast Guard vessels continued the search. They were now at least temporarily accompanied by a ferry carrying relatives of the American and Japanese and South Korean passengers who had died on the plane. The bereaved would pay their last respects at sea as close as possible to the place where it was thought the fuselage of the aircraft had struck the ocean's surface.

The matter of retaliation by the Japanese began to surface on Monday and Tuesday of the week of September 5. There was talk of curtailing social contacts between Soviet officials and Japanese diplomats in Moscow and rumors that the supply of fuel to Soviet airliners landing in Japan would be cut off.

As September 6 began, there had yet to be an admission by the Soviet Union that they had shot down the KAL 747. However, in a TASS statement the Soviets finally admitted that "the interceptor-fighter of the antiaircraft defense fulfilled an order from the command post to stop its flight."

What western military observers and media missed in that statement is that, operationally, the Soviet Air Defense Forces consist of a Central Command Post, two ADF districts and the regions, of which Biya is one. The "command post" referred to in the TASS statement could well have meant Moscow headquarters. But more about that when the question "Who gave the order?" is examined later.

This reluctant admission by the Soviets that they had destroyed the 747 was, of course, a complete reversal of their original position on September 1 when they said Flight 007 had "continued its flight in the direction of the Sea of Japan." On the other hand, the Soviet propagandists would probably say that that was not a lie because what was left of the aircraft at 35,000 feet when it was destroyed by the two missiles did in fact carry on "its flight" toward – and into – the Sea of Japan.

On Wednesday, September 7, through White House spokesman Larry Speakes, the Reagan Administration went out of its way to say that Japan had tapes of some transmissions from Soviet ground-control positions, but that if the tapes were going to be made public it would be up to the Japanese to do so. In any event, the United States did not have any tapes of communications between the Soviet ground-control stations and the Soviet fighter aircraft. The question whether the order to shoot came from the ground was later resolved when 805, the SU-15 pilot, admitted in an interview that the definite order had come from Deputat. That was later confirmed by Marshal Ogarkov at his press conference. But, as of September 6, the question was still alive.

The White House statement was confirmed at the Tuesday, September 6, press conference in Tokyo when Chief Cabinet Secretary Gotoda said that the government had in its possession taped messages from the Soviet ground control to the SU-15 pilot, but that it had chosen not to release them.

The situation became still more confused, however, when the Japanese Defense Agency immediately categorically denied having such tapes. This contradicted the first JDA release, on September 2, of what it claimed was a transcript of the discussion between Soviet ground control and the fighter aircraft.

It is sufficient to say that, at the time of writing, the second tape or tapes – if they exist – have not been made public. It is very likely that they do exist but that the Japanese government had decided not to put its security at risk by releasing them. With regard to the tapes that *were* released, the chief Foreign Ministry spokesman, Wasuke Miyake, told reporters at another of the plethora of press conferences, this one on September 8, that "we are very worried for security reasons about the possible results of revealing these tapes."

At any event, neither the "second tapes" nor the bodies

trapped in the remains of Flight 007 somewhere in the Sea of Japan have surfaced.

The public tapes were, of course, dramatically played by the United States at a special meeting of the United Nations on Tuesday, September 6. The immediate effect was that the Soviets were finally backed into a corner and had to admit that they had indeed shot down Flight 007. It took five excruciatingly long days to get them into that position. It was the tape that did it, just as it was the tapes that broke President Nixon in the Watergate affair. The voices and the words on the tapes – and the responsibility they implied – could not be denied.

The eighth of September brought an announcement by the Soviet Ambassador to Japan, Vladimir Y. Pavlov, that the Russian Navy had discovered more debris from Flight 007. The find had been in international waters. Pavlov's government had arranged to turn the recovered materials and documents over to Japanese officials rather than to South Korea, since there were no diplomatic relations between the U.S.S.R. and South Korea. Tokyo had agreed to be South Korea's agent in the matter.

As to the request by Japan and the United States to enter Soviet waters to continue the search, the Ambassador said that the Soviets "consider it unnecessary at this moment because nothing has been found in the Soviet waters. If the search in Soviet waters becomes necessary, we will study the request again."

As previously mentioned, Pavlov had earlier announced that debris had been discovered in four separate areas to the north of Moneron Island.

Also on September 8, the Japanese government stated that it was looking at possible sanctions against the Soviet Union. The U.S. Ambassador to Japan, Mike Mansfield, had met Foreign Minister Abe to talk about an American proposal for joint reprisals against the Soviet Union. About the precise nature of those measures an announcement would be made "in the nearest future, but not today."

The reprisals the government was rumored to be considering had to do mainly with restricting Aeroflot operations into Japan, and with a public campaign to persuade Japanese citizens not to use the Soviet air carrier in travelling to Europe. But, in cautious Japanese fashion, caught as it was between the rock and the hard place, the government had as yet made no decision on reprisals.

The small armada of non-Soviet ships undertaking the search in the Sea of Japan included: four ships from the Japanese Fisheries Agency and ten Japanese Navy patrol boats; two U.S. Navy vessels, including one specializing in recovery; and a large clutch of South Korean fishing boats, in addition to the Japanese fishing craft that normally populate the area. In the air were some American P3-C reconnaissance aircraft and HC-130 helicopters.

The black boxes were still elusive, but their pinging signals would soon be picked up.

On the ninth day after the event, it was reported that a piece from the 747's tailfin had been found, providing concrete evidence that the missile had exploded in the tail section.

The child's body discovered in the water and the other material found on the beaches were in most unexpected locations. The beaches are near Mobetsu, which is on Hokkaido to the east of La Pérouse Strait and on the Sea of Okhotsk, not the Sea of Japan. The child's body and the pieces of wreckage, including the section of tailfin ripped out by the explosion, were found as much as two hundred miles from where the plane was attacked over Sakhalin Island. The other material found – an oxygen mask, a sponge cushion and a piece of heat-insulating material – was also lightweight. When the tremendous force of the rocket hit the tail section, it must have blasted these objects higher into the thin air. They would then have been carried some distance further than other, heavier debris, in a southeasterly direction, borne by the strong 45-knot wind from the northwest. As bits and pieces descended, their velocities depending on their individual weight and aerodynamic quality, they could have been lifted from time to time by rising air currents, particularly as they crossed the high ground of Sakhalin Island. It was a long six-mile ride down to the surface of the Earth for a fluttering piece of lightweight material that has any lift-producing surface of its own.

The wreckage scattered across the night sky over the Sea of Japan spread out over an incredibly wide area, probably in the range of one hundred miles. The small fragments and light material that floated southeastward into the Sea of Japan were then carried by strong currents through the La Pérouse Strait into the Sea of Okhotsk.

The Cabinet of Prime Minister Yasuhiro Nakasone finally decided what reprisals it would take against the Soviets. There had been much controversy in the cabinet and great concern that, if the sanctions were too strong, the Russians would retaliate. Some members of the cabinet wanted to revoke all Japanese landing rights for Aeroflot, but they were outvoted on the grounds that the Soviets might reciprocate by prohibiting all Japan Air Lines flights into the Soviet Union. There was concern for other interests that might be affected by Soviet retaliation – Japanese fishing operations in certain Soviet rivers, for example.

The result was that the imposed sanctions were not severe. They were all against Aeroflot. Japanese government officials would be prevented from using the Soviet airline. Aeroflot's privilege of operating perhaps five to ten non-scheduled charter flights a year to Japan would be revoked and the airline would not be allowed to increase the number of its scheduled flights into Japan.

Once again, the matter of the second tape, that of the messages from the ground-control operators to the Soviet fighters, raised its head. The newspapers claimed that the government did have the tapes, but again the government stonewalled. There would be no admission.

On Saturday, September 10, a special seventy-day session of the Japanese parliament began. Prime Minister Nakasone's speech was unusual in that it singled out the 747 massacre when, as a general rule, the Prime Minister's opening speech deals with general principles and the broad directions in which the government wishes to take its policies. In his speech, he called the destruction of the South Korean passenger aircraft "an affront to humanity," saying that "Japan must deal firmly with such behavior." His goal was to have a "tenacious dialogue" with the Soviet Union in all matters at issue between them. At the same time, he said, he desired a stable relationship based on mutual understanding.

Nakasone then stated the fundamental principle upon which the Japanese government wanted to continue to act. It wished to be friends with everyone: "Japan thus intends to maintain and develop good relations with all countries of the world and to contribute positively to the economic, cultural and political spheres."

For a country that imports almost all of its raw materials, exports finished products and maintains the highest trade surplus of any nation in the world, that kind of political as well as economic goal was much to be desired.

The case of the second tape continued on its confusing way. In a September 13 press conference, Foreign Ministry spokesman Wasuke Miyake said that Chief Cabinet Secretary Gotoda's earlier statement the the government had the second tapes was incorrect. As Mr. Miyake said: "At that time Mr. Gotoda wasn't quite sure of the fact and denied it after. Now I confirm his denial."

Another issue dealt with by Mr. Miyake at the press conference had to do with a statement by the daily newspaper, *Yomiuri Shimbun*, that Japanese policemen at the beach on northern Hokkaido had "recovered a piece of metal pierced with holes apparently made by machine-gun bullets." Following the confirmation by the Soviet Su-15 pilot that he had fired four rounds of tracers, the question was whether or not the shells had hit the aircraft. But, through spokesman Miyake, the Japanese government refused to confirm or deny the newspaper allegation. Miyake said, "We have 381 pieces under police control. We are now checking, examining. We cannot possibly come to a conclusion at this time."

On Tuesday, September 13, the Japanese govern nent decided to go the final distance in its retaliation against the Soviets. For two weeks, starting on Thursday, September 15, as an additional protest measure, the daily Aeroflot Moscow-Tokyo and the once-a-week Khabarovsk-Niigata flights were cancelled. As a consequence, Japan Air Lines' thrice-weekly flights to Europe via Moscow were also cancelled for the same period. On Wednesday, September 14, Ambassador Pavlov refused to accept Japan's demand for damages for its nationals killed aboard Flight 007. At about the same time the Japanese House of Representatives unanimously passed a resolution condemning the Soviet shooting down of Flight 007. The resolution called the aircraft's destruction "an inhuman act that ignored customs of international civil aviation and international laws, and a totally inexcusable act of brutality from the standpoint of security of international civil aviation."

Meanwhile, the intense search for the black boxes was still going on in the Sea of Japan off Sakhalin Island, with the main players – the Soviet Union, the United States and Japan – combing the area near Moneron Island. Using, among other things, a small submarine, the Soviets were hunting for sections of the aircraft. The U.S. Navy had dispatched a specially equipped tugboat to join a growing U.S. flotilla that included a destroyer, a frigate and a cutter. All were hoping that their special equipment would pick up the distinctive electronic pinging from the underwater acoustical-locator beacon, a water-activated sonar device designed to assist in finding the aircraft's flight data recorder under water. The beacon's water-activated battery would produce power for about thirty days. Signals from it could be detected by a helicopter trailing a sonar buoy or by a surface vessel or a submarine. The range of the pinging signal was no more than five miles.

The area being searched was mountainous, with peaks about 300 feet below the surface and valleys as deep as 2,400 feet.

Soviet ships reported to be in the search area and at work

included the *Petropavlovsk*, a guided-missile cruiser, and the *Georgi Kozumin*, a 12,000-ton rescue ship. On September 17 the latter was observed putting a twenty-foot yellow submarine into the water. After the submarine had completed its subsurface operations it was retrieved by the mother ship, which then dropped red buoys as markers. The Soviet oilwell driller ship, *Mikhail Mirchank*, one of twenty-six Soviet ships operating in the search sector, was later observed hauling up an unidentifiable object from another Soviet ship, causing speculation among observers that it might be the 747's flight recorder.

Also part of the Soviet fleet were one rescue ship, four coast surveillance boats, four minesweepers, four patrol ships, two ocean oil surveyors and nine trawlers.

Among the American craft nearby were the destroyer *Stark*, the fleet ocean tug *Narragansett*, the frigate *Badger*, the specially equipped salvage vessel *Conserver* and the coastguard cutter *Munro*.

In addition, some twenty Japanese ships and sixteen aircraft were searching the surface of the Sea of Japan and the Sea of Okhotsk for debris and bodies.

From the massive effort both the Soviets and the United States were putting into the search for the black boxes, it was clear that each side considered it enormously important that they be found. If the Soviets found the boxes first would they release the information in them? Not if it harmed the Soviet case – as, for example, if the boxes disclosed that there had been no signals given by the Soviet Su-15 pilot, or that he had been instructed to fire his cannon *at* the aircraft, rather than as a warning near it.

And if the Americans found the boxes, would they release the information? They would probably give out the information if, as with the Soviets, what they found did not harm their case and did not affect the civil liability of Korean Air Lines. For example, if the tapes disclosed that the Korean captain and co-pilot heard transmissions from the Soviets on the emergency frequency of 121.5 megacycles, or that they did see the tracer shells, what then?

As the search for the black boxes intensified, the hunt for debris also continued. Five bodies had now been found.

There was great excitement in the American search fleet on Monday, September 19. The tug *Narragansett* and the salvage ship *Conserver* had made intermittent contact with the pinging of the flight data recorder signal box. They had it for about an hour, lost it, then got it back again for half an hour. The recorder was believed to be in about 2,500 feet of water. For a time, then, there was hope that the black boxes would be found by the Americans. But, if the technical information was right, there was only about ten days' power left in the signal box. There was no time to lose.

If the Soviet search fleet had its way, the United States would not succeed. Vessels of the Russian fleet were making every effort to hamper the American search, harassing U.S. ships whenever possible by interfering with the set pattern that the U.S. ships towing locators or sonar devices were sailing. The pattern required sailing back and forth in straight legs over some miles. The Soviets would stop astride a U.S. ship's return leg. This would compel the U.S. ship to get off the straight leg in order to sail around the Soviet ship so that the underwater gear would miss a portion of the search area. Another device the Soviets were using was to sail on parallel courses close to the search ships so that the noise from the Russian propellers and engines would mask and cover the pinging sound of the signal box. The U.S. government protested to the Soviet Embassy in Washington that, under a United States agreement with the Soviet Union, neither side was supposed to train guns on the other, fly military aircraft over the other's ships, interfere with the other's maneuvers, or sail on a possible collision course with the other's ships. Of course, the protest was ignored.

The hostile confrontation between Moscow and Washington had found its way to the Sea of Japan, the place where there could be a head-on physical confrontation as the tension heated up.

The Soviets were about to make a conciliatory gesture, but

it would be done with a grim face. On Tuesday, September 20, they informed the Japanese government that they would hand over "items and documents" that Soviet search teams had found. Delivery would be at Nevelsk on the western coast of Sakhalin. The date would be the following Monday.

During an Upper House Budget Committee session on Wednesday, September 21, Prime Minister Nakasone said that the Sea of Okhotsk was strategically and tactically more important to the Soviet Union than other nations, including Japan, had previously believed. He described the Sea of Okhotsk as the Soviets' "inland sea." Nakasone told the committee that he had formed this opinion after Marshal Ogarkov had explained the Soviet position on the shooting down of the South Korean 747. The Prime Minister noted that Ogarkov had said that the Kamchatka Peninsula was the location of "a major base of the Soviet Union's nuclear forces." It was clear that the Japanese Prime Minister was telling his nation that the Soviet threat to the north of Japan was growing rapidly. His warning was designed to promote a national consensus that would support his government's build-up of its defense forces.

The American search fleet had not been able to start its hunt until September 15, two full weeks after the event. The main reason for the delay was that the task force came from various ports as far away as California and the Philippines. As of September 20, the huge supply ship *Wichita* and the guided missile destroyer *Callaghan* had arrived. The underwater search equipment being used included sonar, towed locators for the detection of pinging sounds and a deep-water drone device that could take photographs of a find.

The Russian search fleet had been reduced from about forty to about sixteen or seventeen ships and the harassment by the Soviets was being reduced.

So was the opportunity to find the black boxes, because time was running out on the pinging signal device. By

September 24, the searchers had probably less than a week until the signal box went dead. After that it would be game over in the attempt to find the small black boxes in a 1,600 square mile area over an undersea mountain range.

So the search carried on, with, now, six ships from the United States, eighteen from Japan, seventeen from the Soviet Union and a research vessel and four trawlers out of South Korea.

The Soviet harassment had eased, but it wasn't over. Shortly after noon on Friday, September 23, a guided-missile destroyer that had joined the Soviet flotilla the day before, along with a smaller ship, approached the *Narragansett* and the *Conserver* as they were on a search leg heading northeast. Meanwhile, the U.S. coastguard cutter *Munro*, which was pulling a drone underwater on a lengthy wire, had to use flag signals to turn away a Soviet ship that had approached within two nautical miles. The signals warned that the *Munro* was carrying out restricted underwater operations. In addition to these interferences, several Soviet aircraft overflew the American flotilla at low level.

In spite of the harassment, the Americans were continuing their all-out effort to pick up the pinging signals and to find the two black boxes. By this time both fleets were using minisubmarines in the hope of beating the inexorable run of the time clock.

On Sunday, September 25, as previously arranged by the Soviets, a solemn, grim-faced group, the Soviets on the one side and a party of Japanese and U.S. government officials and U.S. Navy personnel on the other, faced each other at the fishing port of Nevelsk on the southwest side of Soviet-held Sakhalin Island.

The Soviets had demanded that the Japanese patrol ship *Tsugaru* be stripped of its guns, and its helicopter removed. No representatives of South Korea or Korean Air Lines were permitted to be present because there were no diplomatic relations between the Soviet Union and South Korea. That prompted a protest from the United States that South Korea should be represented because KAL was the owner of the aircraft and South Korea had authorized the United States and Japan exclusively to conduct the search and "no other country had that authority." The response was typical of the Soviets. It was nothing.

The *Tsugaru* docked in Nevelsk, where officials were waiting to hand over five crates of debris. There were no handshakes, no greetings, no smiles, just the cold solemn Soviet faces.

The exchange was done as quickly as possible.

Once back on the *Tsugaru* with the crates, and departing Nevelsk harbor, the group began opening the boxes. There were no human remains. The Soviets had claimed that they had found no human remains whatsoever.

There were some seventy-six objects in the crates: pieces of the aircraft, fuselage, a torn red-and-orange plastic life boat, seat cushions, oxygen cylinders, clothing, shoes and other items, such as a Boeing 747 technical manual, a business contract and various other papers and magazines. There was no flight data recorder and no cockpit voice recorder.

The *Tsugaru* stopped at Wakkanai briefly to show the material to the news media. After being inspected there, the crates were finally taken to Chitose air base on Hokkaido where relatives would be able to see and, it was hoped, identify personal articles.

As this exchange was going on, ships of the United States Seventh Fleet continued their round-the-clock search for the black boxes and the telltale ping from the underwater locator beacon. Time was running out. The batteries were expected to run down in about four days.

New rumors about the finding of the black boxes circulated in Tokyo on September 27. What triggered the belief that the boxes had been found was the boarding that day of American search ships by observers from ICAO and by Japanese officials. The American assumption would be that since anything found by U.S. ships would be discredited as fraudulent by the Soviet authorities, it would be prudent to have independent witnesses if the boxes were found. ICAO, an agency operating under the aegis of the United Nations, and of which the U.S.S.R. is a member, would be the ideal body to confirm the identity of the black boxes and that the Americans had not tampered with the find before the tapes were played back.

Again, the excitement over the possible finding of a black box was transmitted by the media to points around the world, notwithstanding the clear statement by the press attaché at the U.S. Embassy in Tokyo that, "We have not found it."

This was confirmed by a U.S. Navy spokesman in Japan. He was even more emphatic when he said, "As of this afternoon, we have not found the black box. I am not waffling on that one." Even President Reagan got into the act when reporters in Washington asked him whether the U.S. Navy had recovered the recorders, saying that he was the man who should know. His reply: "I have no knowledge that we have. No."

But if the black boxes had not yet been found, why had the ICAO people and Japanese witnesses gone aboard the American ships? The answer came at a press conference in Washington when White House spokesman Larry Speakes announced, "We have narrowed the area of search," and revealed that the Navy had heard the pinging noise. A State Department spokesman said that the search "has been focused on a 14-square-nautical-mile area in which the Navy feels it has the best probability of picking up another signal from the black box, if it is still transmitting."

It was clear that the Navy had decided that it was getting close. It was also clear that it was "now or never", because the power in the acoustic locator beacon would soon give out. So the ICAO and Japanese representatives were brought on board only in the expectation that the finding of a black box, known in Japan as the *buraku bokusu*, might be imminent. By October 4, the U.S. Navy was still bravely pressing on with its search, even though the time limit for the power supply of the acoustic locator beacon had gone by.

In fact, the pinging had died. The U.S. Navy was continuing its underwater search in what would have to be described as a hunt for a needle in a haystack by a man whose eyesight was so bad he had to wear thick glasses . . . and he had just lost the glasses. Seven U.S. Navy ships were still there, patrolling back and forth, relying on video equipment as well as sonar gear. The sonar equipment, with its high-frequency sound waves, registered vibrations bounced back from such underwater objects as ships or, as was hoped, what was left of the rear area of the fuselage and the tail of the Korean 747.

However, the evidence of the tail piece that had already been found strongly suggested that the tail had been blown to pieces and was scattered across a wide area. Whether the two black boxes and the acoustic locator beacon could have survived the massive blast was open to question. It was also questionable whether the beacon was still next to the flight data recorder and had not been blasted apart from it. There was a good possibility that it might be miles away from it.

As the fruitless October days went by, the search continued in extremely difficult weather. It became apparent that the black boxes could not be found.

As the month moved toward its end, fewer and fewer ships – American, Soviet or Japanese – were seen in the waters.

By early November, all were gone.

Neither the Soviet Union nor the United States of America had found a *buraku bokusu*.

Or had they?

12

THE AMERICAN REACTION
TO THE EVENT

IT WAS Secretary of State George P. Shultz who let the people of the United States of America and, for that matter, the rest of the world outside of the Soviet bloc, know that a Soviet fighter had shot down a Korean Air Lines 747 jumbo jet. He did so, his emotions on his sleeve, at a press conference convened by his staff on the morning of September 1.

In the usual way, Mr. Shultz made an opening statement. It was brief and to the point. In it he outlined the event with such precision – describing the actions of the Soviet fighter pilot down to the minute – that the veracity of what he was saying appeared to be indisputable – except, of course, to the Soviets.

His statement was based on the confirmed translation of the Soviet fighter pilot's taped responses to his ground controller as recorded by the Japanese Maritime Safety Agency. But Secretary Shultz gave no indication of his source. He simply let everybody know that he knew exactly what he was talking about. Two short paragraphs show the stunning detail that he delivered without any attribution:

A Soviet pilot recorded visual contact with the aircraft at 18:12 hours. The Soviet plane was, we know, in constant contact with its ground control.

At 18:21 hours the Korean aircraft was reported by the Soviet pilot at 10,000 meters. At 18:26 hours the Soviet pilot reported that he fired a missile and the target was destroyed. At 18:30 hours the Korean aircraft was reported by radar at 5,000 meters. At 18:38 hours the Korean plane disappeared from the radar screen. [The more accurate timing for the disappearance was 18:29 hours; Shultz was simply repeating the information given to him.]

Shultz concluded his prepared statement to the shocked members of the press gallery by detailing what his first formal reaction toward the Soviet Union was and then characterizing America's description of the event. That morning he had called in the Soviet chargé d'affaires to express the nation's grave concern over the shooting down of an unarmed civilian plane and had urgently demanded an explanation. "The United States reacts with revulsion to this attack. Loss of life appears to be heavy. We can see no excuse whatsoever for this appalling act."

"Revulsion" from the appalling act was the key word around which the U.S. reaction, as represented both by Shultz and by the President, grew and developed over the next days and weeks.

In the question and answer period that followed Mr. Shultz's delivery of this statement (during which this normally phlegmatic man's voice occasionally rose in anger), only ten questions were asked. A curious pair of answers were given to one question:

Q. Have you spoken to the President about this matter and what did he say?

A. I haven't spoken to the President as yet. But I should say, the President was fully informed, and I've talked to the West Coast, and the President knows all about this and has been kept fully informed. I haven't personally spoken to him.

What Secretary Shultz meant was that he had talked by telephone with William P. Clark, at the time the President's

National Security Advisor, and Edwin Meese III, the White House Counsellor, both of whom were at the Santa Barbara Biltmore, a resort hotel about twenty miles from the President's ranch in the California mountains where he and his wife were taking one of their many brief vacations. Shultz had been assured by Clark and Meese that they had briefed the President. It was, of course, around 6:00 a.m. California time, or perhaps even earlier, when Shultz decided to move on the firm information he then had.

It is instructive to note that his relationship with Reagan on the one hand and with Meese and Clark on the other was such that he felt compelled to deal with the Clark/Meese team rather than call the President directly. Perhaps there was a rule about not calling the President so early in the morning. Perhaps it was the President's edict that Clark and Meese could make decisions for him on the basis that they would inform him later no matter how serious the crisis. Whatever, the KAL 747 event was indeed a crisis requiring immediate strong action.

However as the record showed, Shultz had not spoken to the President. The President had not authorized what he had said by way of a statement, but rather was "fully informed." That meant he had been listening, not ordering or approving.

Reagan was not informed until 7:10 a.m. (10:10 a.m. New York time) that the plane had been shot down. Larry Speakes, the chief White House spokesman, said that Clark had been briefed by Shultz nearly two hours before. It was only shortly after the President was told that the aircraft had been destroyed that Mr. Shultz announced the event at the State Department press conference. It was clear that Mr. Shultz was making a statement without the President's having approved it. If anyone had approved it other than Shultz himself, it could only have been Meese and/or Clark. Interesting.

This incident clearly demonstrates that President Reagan had great confidence in his Secretary of State. It also demonstrates that he had total confidence both in Judge William Clark, and in Ed Meese, his White House Counsellor (now Attorney General).

This apparent lack of direction by the President and the possibility that it might attract editorial attention was probably the reason that Clark and Meese constructed the "White House" statement that day and issued it from Santa Barbara. They took pains to explain the extent of the President's knowledge of the situation:

> The President discussed this matter last night at 7:30 with his national security advisor, Bill Clark, and again at 10:30 last night he was briefed in further detail. This morning at 7:10 a.m., Ed Meese spoke to the President, providing him with a morning assessment of the situation, and at 8:33 this morning the President spoke for about 15 minutes with Secretary Shultz.

Those are California times, three hours behind Washington. Shultz spoke with the President *after* the Secretary's press conference.

That Santa Barbara statement merely said that the President was very concerned and deeply disturbed about the loss of life aboard the Korean Air Lines flight. However, as the day wore on, Reagan, Clark and Meese got a better feel for the situation and prepared to come out with a much stronger statement.

Meanwhile back where the action really was, in Washington, the Soviet Foreign Minister, Andrei A. Gromyko, had sent a message to his counterpart, George Shultz, that was similar to the brief disclaimer issued by TASS earlier that day, admitting an interception over Soviet airspace but disclaiming Soviet responsibility by saying that Flight 007 "continued its flight in the direction of the Sea of Japan." He responded to the urgent American request for further information, saying that Soviet search aircraft had discovered "signs of a possible crash" near Moneron Island. The

State Department rejected this explanation as inadequate and reaffirmed its demand for a satisfactory explanation. They would have to wait a long time, and the explanation that finally did emerge was never satisfactory.

Secretary Shultz was scheduled to be in Madrid the following week for a meeting of East-West Foreign Ministers. Would the 747 event cause him to cancel a planned meeting there with Gromyko? The answer was emphatically no. It was the first question put to him at the press conference that morning. "I certainly will want to meet with Foreign Minister Gromyko and hear what he has to say about this," he replied.

State Department officials were attempting to characterize the 747 event as an "international" rather than an American-Soviet matter. This interpretation was either wishful thinking or an early basic mistake in comprehending the seriousness of the situation. The second TASS statement, which was put out later that day, removed any doubt that it would be an American-Soviet issue when it claimed that the intrusion of the KAL 747 into Soviet airspace could not be "regarded in any other way than as a preplanned act" which was to "attain special intelligence aims without hindrance using civilian planes as a cover." TASS cited the U.S. Central Intelligence Agency, saying "U.S. services followed the flight throughout its duration in the most attentive manner." The allegation was clear. KAL Flight 007 was over Soviet airspace on an intelligence mission for the American CIA. That was only the opening Soviet shot in what would turn out to be a fusillade.

The great 747 "massacre," as President Reagan and others were later to describe it, would be first and foremost an American-Soviet issue, in addition to being an "international" one.

With the strong statement of Secretary Shultz came a series of questions concerning American-Soviet relations.

Would the United States go ahead with the U.S.-U.S.S.R. arms-control talks on medium-range missiles that were scheduled to resume in Geneva the following week? An agreement there might obviate the necessity of deploying American Pershing 2 and cruise missiles in Europe later in the year.

What would happen to the long-term grain deal signed with the Soviet Union just the week before, under which the U.S.S.R. had agreed to buy 500,000 tons of wheat, and 400,000 tons of corn for some $150 million? The first sale under that agreement had been announced by the Department of Agriculture that very day.

Would the President respond to conservative reaction and demands that the United States should protest in a strong as possible non-military terms? There were calls to suspend arms-control negotiations, to suspend all American trade with the Russians, to sever diplomatic ties, to recall the United States Ambassador from Moscow and to expel Soviet personnel from the United States. Would the President buy this kind of action?

The man who would have to answer these questions was at his ranch in California. He was now giving the situation his full attention.

As events escalated during the morning of Thursday, September 1, President Reagan made some decisions. He would cut short his vacation by two days. He convened a National Security Council meeting for Friday evening to review the situation and discuss options. He would invite Congressional leaders of both parties to meet with him and his officials at the White House on Sunday for a briefing. And he would make a full-blown statement of his own that afternoon.

President Reagan's decision to return to the White House early came as a surprise in that, earlier in the day, White House officials had said publicly that he would not do so because he was fully capable of having detailed discussions with his advisors from his Santa Barbara ranch. However, the information from the tapes of the Soviet fighter pilots was available; the intention of the Soviet government to accuse the United States of an espionage involvement with Flight 007 was becoming clearer; the public might misinterpret the President's decision to continue his vacation; a thorough discussion of the situation with the National Security Council was necessary; and it was important to get the Congressional leaders of both the Republican and the Democratic parties briefed and onside. These were all factors that would have been taken into consideration by the President, Clark and Meese.

When the three of them finally put it together, the President's statement was even stronger than George Shultz's earlier one. The President accused the Soviet Union of committing a "barbaric act" against a commercial jetliner. He rhetorically asked what could be thought of a regime that "so callously and quickly commits a terrorist act" and questioned "what could be said about Soviet credibility when they so flagrantly lie about such a heinous act?" He characterized the event as an atrocity and called for an urgent U.N. Security Council meeting so that the "brutality of this action" would not be compounded.

The President of the United States had hit hard. The Soviet response was the second TASS statement in which for the first time the U.S.S.R. linked the CIA and the U.S. government to alleged espionage purposes for Flight 007.

In the TASS statement of September 2, the Soviet government struck back as strongly as it could. After saying that there was reason to believe that those who organized the (747 intrusion) provocation were striving to smear the Soviet Union, the Soviet government said: "This is illustrated also by the impudent, slanderous statement in respect of the Soviet Union that was instantly made by President Reagan of the United States." It then concluded with: ". . . a resolute condemnation of those [President Reagan and George Shultz, who else?] who consciously or as a result of criminal disregard have allowed the death of people and are now trying to use this occurrence for unseemly political aims."

The American Eagle and the Russian Bear had joined in battle. The allegations and counter-allegations, the claims and counter-claims, the propaganda and counter-propaganda – all of these would fly in a word-war that would bring the people of the non-communist world to the edges of their chairs.

Speculation immediately turned to what retaliatory steps the President might take in addition to cancelling the wheat deal, withdrawing from the arms talks and not allowing Shultz to go to Madrid.

A major consideration was that the 747 was a Korean aircraft and not an American-operated machine. Furthermore the event took place thousands of miles away from the United States. It was true that many American nationals had died, including a member of Congress, Larry McDonald. But the need or opportunity for retaliation was not nearly so obvious as it would have been had the aircraft been one of Pan Am's, or another U.S. carrier's and the bulk of the people on board U.S. citizens. The retaliatory steps and the reaction of the United States in that scenario take the mind beyond the boggling point.

In fact the President had used up most of his sanctions. He could not cut off Aeroflot because he had already done that after the imposition of martial law in Poland in December 1981. As for cutting off equipment and other supplies for the great Soviet gas pipeline – he had already used that one, too. Pan American World Airways, the only U.S. carrier that had been flying from the U.S. to Moscow, had long since terminated its service because it was uneconomical.

What he could do was ask that Asian and European allies suspend all flights to and from the Soviet Union for a limited period of, say, sixty to ninety days as a combined demonstration of international anger.

Canada was the first off the mark, on its own initiative and without any prompting from the United States. On Monday, September 5, the Canadian Minister of External Affairs, Allan MacEachen, announced that the weekly Aeroflot flight from Moscow into Mirabel Airport in Montreal would be cancelled. Canada had fewer nationals on board the 747 than the United States – eight Canadians as against sixty-one U.S. nationals.

Other steps that Reagan could take were to: end all ongoing cultural and scientific exchanges with the Soviet Union; end all trade with the Soviet Union; and deny Soviet ships access to all U.S. ports. He could also adopt the recommendations of the Conservative Caucus, a group of strong, right-wing organizations that had actively supported the Reagan campaign in 1980. The caucus demanded the recall of the U.S. Ambassador to Moscow and, among other things, the expulsion of all Soviet personnel from the United States.

The obvious question about each of these proposals was: What good would it do?

President Reagan returned to the White House on Friday, September 2, accompanied by Meese and Clark. He spoke in California before flying back to Washington for a meeting of the National Security Council that evening. In the presence of television and other media, he took his second shot at the Soviets. "Words can scarcely express our revulsion at this horrifying act of violence," he said, and demanded a full explanation for this appalling and wanton misdeed. Those were extremely harsh words for the head of one nation to be saying about the actions of another country. Reagan was angry, and rightly so, since the Soviets so far were refusing even to acknowledge that they had shot the 747 down, let alone that they were responsible.

As the President was winging back to Washington, Secretary Shultz angrily responded to the TASS statement that had been released on the evening of Thursday, September 1. This, was TASS's "hullabaloo" text excoriating the President. The Soviets had still not admitted they had attacked Flight 007. This upset Shultz again. His statement was extremely critical of them. It finished with the position that the Secretary of State and, it is implied, the President as well wanted to get across to the world: "No cover-up, however . . . elaborate can . . . absolve the Soviet Union of responsibility to explain its behavior. The world is waiting for the Soviet Union to tell the truth."

The world had to wait a long time for the Soviets to admit they had shot down the KAL 747. It is still waiting for the Soviet Union to tell the truth.

In his meeting with the National Security Council at the White House on the evening of Friday, September 2, attended by, among others, Secretary Shultz, Defense Secretary Caspar Weinberger and General John Vesey, chairman of the Joint Chiefs of Staff, the President had a full-scale briefing, as did his National Security Advisor, Judge Clark. They heard the tape of the Soviet pilot and the translation, which, a few days later, was to be amended, causing some embarrassment to the United States and giving a major propaganda advantage to the Soviets.

The main concern of the meeting was to consider the options that could be used as a response to the Soviet action. What retaliatory action could the United States take, either alone or, better still, in collaboration with its allies? How could the Russians be punished and what steps could be taken to ensure that a "heinous" incident like this would not be repeated? There was no question that hopes for significant advances for arms negotiations would be cool for some time to come and that the chance of a summit conference with Andropov was now non-existent.

It was also clear to the President and his advisors that the 747 incident would strengthen the President's case for Congress to provide additional money for the defense budget and, in particular, for the MX missile, the new-generation intercontinental ballistic missile program. The incident would also give a psychological advantage to the western-European governments that had decided, despite well-organized, large-scale protest, to deploy the U.S. Pershings and cruise missiles.

At the National Security Council meeting, the decision was made that there should be a "measured response", particularly since most of the Americans' retaliation cards had already been played. Under the "measured-response" umbrella, the decision was made to maintain the most important links with the Kremlin: Shultz would meet with Soviet Foreign Minister Gromyko in Madrid later in the month; the new American-Soviet grain agreement would go ahead, as would the arms-control talks in Geneva. The President would deal with the 747 incident in his weekend radio broadcast and, most important, there would be thorough preparation for the briefing of the Congressional leaders on Sunday.

It was the "measured-response" decision that was to shape President Reagan's approach, notwithstanding the demands of his ultra-conservative supporters for strong action.

The word that came from the White House on Saturday confirmed that there would be no trade sanctions against the Soviet Union; nor would there be any suspension of the arms-control talks. The objective of the United States would be to find a positive way of dealing with the Soviets rather than simply to attempt to punish them. The objective was to ensure the safety of international travel by, among other things, getting the Soviet Union to enter into an agreement to respect the inviolability of civilian airliners even when they stray over sensitive areas of another country's territory.

In his radio talk to the nation on Saturday, the President was clearly restrained, his language much less dramatic, in his condemnation of the Soviets. The restrained posture he had decided to take was made clear when he said, " It is up to all of us, leaders and citizens of the world, to deal with the Soviets in a calm, controlled but absolutely firm manner. We have joined in this call for an urgent U.N. Security Council meeting."

The decision to convene the U.N. Security Council had already been taken by the United Nations the previous day. There would be an emergency session to consider the destruction of the Korean 747. In addition, a special session of the thirty-three-nation steering committee of ICAO was called to consider a Korean motion that the Soviets be condemned. In the Security Council of the United Nations a Soviet veto could prevent such a condemnation, although that veto would not prevent original passage of such a motion and the debate that preceded it. On the other hand, the Soviets would have no veto in the proceedings of ICAO, either in its steering committee or in its 47-member plenary session.

On Saturday the President met Paul Nitze, the American negotiator responsible for dealing with the Soviets on limiting nuclear missiles in Europe. The President's instructions were clear. Nitze was to resume bargaining in Geneva the following Tuesday because the President thought that "peace is that all-important that we shall continue those talks."

Meanwhile, in Moscow, the Soviets had been working furiously on the preparation of a statement reacting to the harsh words and accusations of Reagan and Shultz. The counter-propaganda machinery was in high gear and the language of the Soviet statement issued through TASS on Saturday, September 3, was emotional and vicious. The United States, not the Soviet Union, was responsible for the deaths of the 269 people on the Korean 747.

> Washington is feverishly covering up traces of the provocation staged against the Soviet Union with the utilization of the South Korean plane.
>
> The White House and Department of State are mounting a world-wide rabid anti-Soviet campaign. The tone is set by the U.S. President in his statement permeated with frenzied hatred and malice for the Soviet state, for socialism. Using as a cover-up bombastic phrases about "humanism" and "noble feelings," the head of the White House is trying to convince public opinion that the U.S.S.R. allegedly is guilty of [causing] loss of life.

The statement went on to quote various newspapers and authorities around the world in an attempt to incriminate the

CIA and the United States and to emphasize that the aircraft had been over top-secret zones of the Soviet Union. Nowhere was there any admission that the Soviet Union had shot down Flight 007. That would come later, when the Soviets were forced into it by the publication of the still-secret tapes of the fighter pilot's reports.

The statement claimed that the Korean Air Lines planes flying the routes near Soviet territory were "manned exclusively by air force pilots," the implication being that the overflight of Soviet territory had been deliberate. There was reference to the Inertial Navigation System and the checks that would make it inconceivable that the aircraft could inadvertently stray from its planned course. And there was the claim that the 747 could be mistaken by radar for "an intelligence plane of the U.S. Air Force or for a U.S. E4B Bomber."

The Soviets had a good point in claiming that the 747 could be mistaken for an E4B. But in the developing controversy over identification of Flight 007 either by the Su-15 or the ground radars, they failed to pursue it.

The E4B is not a bomber, as the Soviets thought. It is a modified Boeing 747 developed in its E4A configuration to carry electronic equipment transferred from the RC-135 aircraft. The three E4A's that were built were to carry out the same function as the RC-135.

The later E4B's also carry out the RC-135 role, but with much more up-to-date and sophisticated electronic equipment.

This intelligence would have been known not only by the radar forces in Kamchatka and Sakhalin but by the Su-15 pilot as well.

Therefore the Soviets might well have claimed that they thought the target was a Boeing E4A or B, a claim that would have given more weight to their failure to identify Flight 007.

While the Soviets were using every effort to make the public believe that the Americans were responsible, and at the same time were still refusing to admit that they had anything to do with the disappearance of the aircraft, President Reagan was saying in his radio broadcast that day that, "The evidence is clear. It leaves no doubt. It is time for the Soviets to account. The Soviet Union owes the world the fullest possible explanation and apology for their inexcusable act of brutality."

There would be no accounting. There would be no apology from a government that believed that it was fully justified in doing what it did, and whose own laws required its action.

On the morning of Sunday, September 4, the President and most of the members of the National Security Council met at the White House with the Congressional leaders. A full briefing was given, including the playing of the tape of the Soviet fighter pilots in their exchanges with their ground control. After hearing those tapes, the Congressional leaders, like the President's advisors, were totally convinced that the Soviets had indeed shot down the Boeing 747.

The President discussed with the Congressional delegation possible sanctions in the areas of air rights, commerce, grain, technology and the alteration of diplomatic relations between the two countries.

He also informed them that a U.S. Air Force reconnaissance aircraft (an RC-135) had been in the area of the Korean 747 as the civilian airliner approached the Kamchatka Peninsula and Soviet airspace.

It was this information that the Soviets did not have up to that point. I have already described its release as the making of, not disinformation, but dumbinformation that caused Senator Byrd to say, "I wish he'd never brought it up."

The President took to the airwaves again on the evening of Monday, September 5. This time he used his most powerful medium television.

At a press briefing before the President's speech, a fact sheet had been distributed on what actions the Administration would be taking against the Soviets. There would be a suspension of discussions aimed at renewing American-Soviet scientific and cultural exchange agreements, in existence since 1958, facilitating exchanges of performing arts groups, museum exhibits and scholarly presentations. A few months before, the Reagan Administration had opened discussions on a new agreement. The old one had expired in 1979, and in 1980 President Carter had suspended renewal discussions after the invasion of Afghanistan by the Soviets.

The fact sheet also disclosed the cancellation of U.S.-Soviet discussions about establishing an American consulate in Kiev and a Soviet consulate in New York City.

An effort was being made to influence other nations to restrict the operations of Aeroflot. In his speech, the President was "pleased to report" that "Canada today suspended Aeroflot's landing and refueling privileges for sixty days." He might have added that Canada had taken the action independently, without pushing from the United States.

In his speech, President Reagan once again condemned the Soviet Union for what he called "the Korean Air Lines massacre" and for an "act of barbarism" that was "not just against ourselves or the Republic of Korea. This was the Soviet Union against the world and the moral precepts which guide human relations among people everywhere."

In retaliation, President Reagan said, "We have notified the Soviets that we will not renew our bilateral agreement for co-operation in the field of transportation so long as they threaten the security of civil aviation." The cancellation of Aeroflot flights to the United States was reaffirmed and, the President said, other steps were being looked at with regard to Aeroflot facilities in the United States. Congress would be asked to pass a joint resolution of condemnation. Negotiations on several bilateral arrangements with the Soviets were to be suspended, and a claim against the Soviet Union would be lodged within the week to obtain compensation for the victims' survivors. The United States would redouble its efforts with its allies to end the flow of military and strategic items to the Soviet Union.

During this address, the tape of the Soviet pilot's voice was first played for the public. After describing the flight of the 747 out of Anchorage, admitting that "it was for a brief time in the vicinity of one of our reconnaissance planes, an RC-135 on a routine mission," and discussing the scrambling of the Soviet jet interceptors from their base on Sakhalin Island, the President had a brief segment of the tape played, saying that the whole of it would be played for the U.N. Security Council the next day.

The effect of playing that small section of the tape, with the President's interpretation of what had been heard, was dramatic. "He says he is locked on to the radar which aims his missiles; he has launched those missiles; the target has been destroyed, and he is breaking off the attack."

The President of the United States had produced incontrovertible proof that the Soviets had shot down the 747.

As to the possibility that the Soviet fighter pilot might have confused the 747 with an RC-135, the President was emphatic:

> Let me point out something here having to do with his close-up view of the airliner on what we know was a clear night with a half moon. The 747 has a unique and distinctive silhouette, unlike any other plane in the world. There is no way a pilot could mistake this for anything other than a civilian airliner. And if that isn't enough, let me point out [that] our RC-135, that I mentioned earlier, had been back at his base at Alaska on the ground for an hour when the murderous attack took place over the Sea of Japan.

What the President failed to say was that the 747 could have been mistaken for a Boeing E4A or B, an electronic intelligence aircraft in the 747's exact contour. Therefore, notwithstanding his claim, it *could* have been mistaken for something other than a civilian airliner. The red herring of the RC-135 had been well and truly thrown into the waiting paws of the surprised Russian Bear. He would know what to do with it. The contentious issue of whether the Soviet pilot could or did identify the aircraft as a 747 would continue to be just that, contentious.

The President of the United States had laid out his position clearly and unequivocally. Now it was time to pass the ball to the United Nations. So far as President Reagan was concerned, the evidence was perfectly clear. The best forum in which to pursue the Soviets was that supposedly neutral body, the United Nations. He advised his watching audience that, "along with Korea and Japan, we called an emergency meeting of the U.N. Security Council which began on Friday [September 2]. On that first day Korea, Japan, Canada, Australia, the Netherlands, Pakistan, France, China, the United Kingdom, Zaire, New Zealand and West Germany, all joined us in denouncing the Soviet action and expressing our horror."

The U.N. debate was to continue the next day, Tuesday, September 6. The planned U.S. tactic at the U.N. was to play the entire tape of the Soviet pilot's transmissions. Perhaps that would paint the Russians into a corner and force them to admit that they had in fact destroyed the Korean 747.

The speech of U.S. Ambassador Jeane Kirkpatrick at the U.N. on Tuesday and, two days later, the performance of Marshal Ogarkov in Moscow were to be the two remaining highlights in the aftermath's war of propaganda words.

13

THE SUPERPOWER BATTLE
IN THE UNITED NATIONS

ON TUESDAY, September 6, the scene shifted to U.N. headquarters in New York and the continuing speeches of condemnation against the Soviet Union. This was the day the United States would have its say. In so doing it would present to the Security Council and to the people of the world a damning and incontrovertible piece of evidence – the Soviet fighter pilot's tape. This would be listened to and the transcript of it would be read by tens of millions of people in countries everywhere in the free world as the United States sought to sway public opinion against the Soviet Union. For its part, the Soviets would attempt to convince that same public that the aircraft was on an electronic espionage mission for the United States, that the Soviets were perfectly justified in shooting it down, and that the responsibility for the death of the passengers and crew rested squarely on the shoulders of the President of the United States and his nation.

During the debate on Friday, September 2, those nations that were appalled by the act and were prepared to believe that the Soviets had shot the 747 down first voiced their outrage. The words "murder" and "massacre" echoed through the Security Council chamber as the representatives of Canada, Australia and the United States made their statements. The Canadian delegate, Gérard Pelletier, said that the shooting down of a "civilian, unarmed, easily identifiable passenger aircraft by the Soviet Union is nothing short of murder." Canada urged an inquiry by the International Civil Aviation Organization and demanded that Moscow compensate the families of the victims.

The Australian deputy delegate, L. L. E. Joseph, said that the incident was "quite simply a massacre in the sky" and that no nation "can be justified in shooting down an unarmed civilian aircraft serving no military purpose."

The worldwide outrage was building.

The deputy delegate of the United States, Charles Lichenstein, alleged that the Russians had committed "wanton, calculated, deliberate murder."

In response the Soviet deputy delegate, Richard Ovinnikov, accused the U.S. of attempting to promote "anti-Soviet hysteria," saying that the calling of a special meeting of the Security Council by the United States, South Korea and Japan "was totally unjustifiable" and that the United States' request was "only a cover," a "type of false coin which they have thrown into the dirty, anti-Soviet game that they are planning." Ovinnikov made other allegations and then made a statement that would help erode the credibility of the United States one week later, claiming that the Soviet planes had fired "warning shots with tracer signals" to let the 747 know it was intruding into Soviet airspace over Sakhalin Island.

When the Security Council session resumed on the morning of Tuesday, September 6, it was to be the day of the United States' major assault on the Soviets. The American delegate to the United Nations, Jeane Kirkpatrick, emphatically stated the American position, supporting her assertions with eleven minutes of the tape-recorded voice of the Soviet fighter pilot who had brought down the Korean 747. As his voice was heard, five television screens distributed around the chamber displayed the translation from Russian to English for the representatives of the Council's fifteen members and other diplomats to read.

Jeane Kirkpatrick effectively captured the meaning of the tapes, which contradicted what the Soviet representatives and TASS had been saying. She said: "It establishes that the

Soviets decided to shoot down a civilian airliner, shot it down and lied about it."

While the tape-recording was being played, the Soviet delegate, Oleg Troyanovsky, sat solemnly staring ahead, a translation earphone clamped to his right ear, his chin on his hand. Not wanting to appear to be paying much attention, he started to pass papers back to one of his men sitting behind him. He would have his words when Kirkpatrick was finished with her lengthy address. In it she read out all the known facts from the American point of view and then spoke in a highly derogatory tone about the Soviets:

> They have spoken as though a plane's straying off course is a crime punishable by death. They have suggested that, like any self-respecting state, they are doing no more than looking after their sovereignty, which they shall permit no one to violate.
>
> They have claimed, still without acknowledging that they shot down the Korean airliner, that "our anti-aircraft defense has fulfilled its duty for the defense of the security of our motherland." They have suggested that they may have mistaken the Korean airliner for an American reconnaissance plane, but still do not admit that they attacked and destroyed it.
>
> But none of these lies, half-lies and excuses can withstand examination.

Ambassador Kirkpatrick had many accusations to make: that the Soviets violated "the norms of civilized conduct on which international aviation rests;" that "violence and lies are regular instruments of Soviet policy;" that "at no point did the pilots raise the question of the identity of the target aircraft, nor at any time did the interceptor pilots refer to it as anything other than the target;" that the Soviets "have callously refused offers of international participation in search and rescue efforts in spite of clearly stated international standards and recommended practices of the International Civil Aviation Organization;" that the Soviet Union is "a state based on the dual principles of callousness and mendacity, dedicated to the rule of force;" and that "contrary to Soviet statements, the pilot makes no mention of firing any warning shots – only the firing of the missiles which, he said, struck the target."

The Kirkpatrick address was a comprehensive, emotional summary of the American position to that moment. It was a reflection of the revulsion that her government felt for the act itself and for the lying and evasive posture of the Soviet Union. So far as Kirkpatrick was concerned, she had caught them in the act.

She concluded by saying that "the United States deeply believes that immediate steps should be taken here in the United Nations to decrease the likelihood of any repetition of the tragedy of K.A.L. 7." What she meant was that the United States, with others, would draft a motion condemning the Soviets. She wanted the support of as many members of the Security Council as she could muster to get that as-yet-unformed motion passed, even though it would undoubtedly be vetoed by the Soviet Union.

Was Soviet delegate Troyanovsky cowed by Kirkpatrick's address, or, for that matter, by the pilot's tape? Not at all. He responded by saying what Moscow had been alleging since the event: that the 747 was off course not by accident but by design, in another of an ongoing series of attempts to spy on Soviet military bases. He asked: "Who is responsible for the downfall of the South Korean plane and who jeopardized the lives of many people?" And he replied: "Not the Soviet Union." He said that the 269 civilians who died were "further victims of the cold war, whose apologist and pursuer is the U.S. Administration." Troyanovsky argued sternly, alleging that the American concern was hypocritical, and that the U.S. military reconnaissance plane and the Korean jet (as revealed by the Reagan Administration) were on a linked mission. He rhetorically asked why the tapes of the South Korean pilots had not been played and why the U.S.

and Japanese ground controllers had failed to get the aircraft back on course when it had strayed over Soviet military installations. He could not believe that the 747's navigational equipment had failed, because there were three computer navigation systems on board.

Neither Troyanovsky nor his government were prepared to back off. The KAL 747 was on a spying mission in concert with the United States. The Soviet Union was fully justified in shooting it down. That was the unswerving party line of the Soviet Union then and it remains so today.

The Kirkpatrick address was the opening gambit in a high-powered U.S. political initiative within the framework of the Security Council. The first objective was to draft a Security Council resolution condemning the Soviet Union for the destruction of the Korean 747. The second was to get the nine votes (out of a possible fifteen) needed to force the Soviet Union to use its veto.

In pursuit of maintaining American public opinion behind the action of the Reagan Administration, it was absolutely essential to have the nine votes. In accordance with Security Council rules, if only eight votes had been for the resolution, the resolution and document would have failed and the negative Soviet vote, which was sure to come, would not have counted as a "veto." The end result would be a resounding political humiliation for the United States. Astonishingly enough, the situation could have developed that way even though it was the Soviet Union that had shot down the 747, not the United States.

The drafting of the proposed motion and, at the same time, lobbying for the support of Third World members of the Council began. It became clear that some of those Third World members might be prepared to condemn the act, but not the nation carrying out the act, and that they might well abstain if the Soviet Union was named.

It was taken for granted by all that the Soviet Union would veto the resolution if need be. What was at stake was political face.

For the United States there were five sure votes, besides its own. These were: Britain, France, the Netherlands, Togo and Zaire. The Soviets were certain of support from Poland. As of September 7, the opinion was that Nicaragua would either vote with Moscow or abstain.

China, Malta, Guyana, Zimbabwe, Jordan and Pakistan were uncertain. Three of them had to go with the U.S. motion or the Reagan Administration would face an embarrassing defeat. Abstention or non-participation could bring about the same result as a negative vote.

Among the drafting group were the Netherlands, France and Britain, with the United States leading and inviting participatory advice from Canada, South Korea, Australia and Japan.

By Friday, September 9, the resolution had been drafted in a way that would allow the Third World nations and China to support it, or so the Americans thought. There was no reference to the Soviet Union in the body of the resolution, although in the preamble to the resolution, the Soviet Union was named as the country that had shot down the Korean Air Lines aircraft. Everything seemed to be set for the United States to see the resolution passed that day.

However, before the opening of the September 9 session, the United States' chief delegate, Kirkpatrick, realized that some of the nations she was counting on for support did not have final instructions from their governments. If forced to vote they would have no choice but to abstain, which would have meant political disaster for the Americans. Guyana, Jordan, Zimbabwe and Malta were among that group. As for China, the Americans had been counting on its support, but on the morning of the ninth were appalled to discover that the Chinese were leaning toward abstention.

Kirkpatrick realized that if the motion was voted on that day the resolution would be lost. Therefore, with the support of America's allies in the cause, she moved to have the Security Council put off the vote until Monday. Ironically, this too put the resolution within a hair's breadth of destruction, when the events of Sunday, September 11, intervened to shake the confidence of America's allies in the Security Council.

In the middle of the lobbying for support that took place over the weekend, the United States was confronted by a reinterpretation of the tapes by U.S. State Department experts. They had reviewed the poor-quality transmissions by the fighter pilot to his ground controller. The result was that their linguists had been "able to interpret three passages more clearly."

Pilot 805's transmission at 18:19:08 GMT, which was originally translated as, "I have enough time," was revised to, "They do not see me."

The second change in the transcript involved a previously unintelligible transmission pilot 805 made just a few seconds later at 18:20:49. When deciphered, the Su-15 pilot's words were, "I am firing cannon bursts." This is exactly what Soviet deputy representative Ovinnikov claimed during the debate on Friday, September 2, a position which had been ridiculed by Kirkpatrick in her address on September 6, when she said "contrary to Soviet statements, the pilot makes no mention of firing any warning shots . . . "

When this shocking admission was made by the United States on Sunday, September 11, it had a profound effect on all the wavering Third World nations that might have gone with the United States and that were apparently prepared to do so up to the time of the announcement.

The third transcript change involved a transmission made at 18:23:37, when the pilot was supposed to have said, "Now I will try a rocket." This was changed to, "Now I will try rockets."

It was the change to "I am firing cannon bursts" that shook the delegates from Nicaragua, Zimbabwe, Guyana and Malta. All of them were concerned with safety and security in international civil aviation and were pleased with the proposal and resolution that the Secretary General of the United Nations should "conduct a full investigation into the circumstances of the tragedy." On the other hand, there was concern that the text was too one-sided or, more importantly, that there were too many unanswered questions. The tape changes called into question the veracity, credibility and strength of the United States' position.

Finally, and virtually at the last minute, the ninth Council member – the tiny state of Malta – its reservations notwithstanding, was persuaded to vote for the resolution. Malta's delegate, Victor Gauchi, agreed to change his decision for abstention and to vote for the motion, despite the belief of his nation, and of Nicaragua, Zimbabwe and Guyana, that by that time the circumstances enveloping the destruction of the Korean 747 had been "clouded with too much uncertainty."

Ambassador Gauchi voted with the United States, Britain, France, the Netherlands, Pakistan, Jordan, Zaire and Togo. The motion was passed. The face of the United States was saved.

It was astonishingly incongruous that, although the Soviet Union had shot down the 747 and killed 269 people, the United States should be on the defensive. The Americans were scrambling to ward off the intensive and effective Soviet counter-propaganda assault. They were suffering from the combined effects of their own ineptitude in announcing the presence of the RC-135 in the area at the time and their State Department translators' initial failure to come up with the correct interpretation of the "cannon" transmission.

The United States had won its battle of politics in the Security Council of the United Nations. It had saved face. But in the process, the credibility of the Soviet Union's position and story had been substantially improved.

The reason for the abstentions was now the pervasive uncertainty as to who was right and who was wrong.

China abstained, according to its delegate, Ling Qing, "in view of the serious dispute over certain aspects of this incident." Even the Malta delegate, Victor Gauchi, the reluctant last vote for the resolution, admitted that the circumstances had been "clouded with too much uncertainty." The Soviet propaganda machine – helped by U.S. mistakes – was making substantial progress in its fight to pin the blame for the 747 massacre on the United States.

In the Security Council debate that day, Troyanovsky repeated the allegation that the airliner had been involved in a spy mission. "No doubt remains," he claimed. There were many now in that Security Council chamber and throughout the western world who believed he might be right.

Two events followed the passing of the Security Council resolution on the Korean airliner and its veto by the Soviet Union. The first came out of Paragraph 6 of the resolution. It invited the Secretary General "making use of such expert advice as he deems necessary and in consultation with appropriate international bodies, to conduct a full investigation into the circumstances of the tragedy."

That invitation was acted on promptly by the U.N.-sponsored International Civil Aviation Organization (ICAO). The ICAO Council met on September 15 and 16, in an Extraordinary Session. A resolution was passed directing its Secretary General to institute an investigation to determine the facts and technical aspects relating to the flight and destruction of Korean Air Lines (KAL) Flight 007 on September 1, 1983, and to provide a final report thereon during the current session.

The ICAO investigation team moved quickly. Its final report, an important, well-researched document, and its various conclusions are dealt with in other parts of this book.

The other event that flowed from the U.S.-Soviet confrontation in the Security Council occurred on September 19 when the whole issue was still hotly boiling between the parties.

What happened was this. Soviet Foreign Minister Andrei Gromyko was to fly to New York from the Soviet Union to attend the U.N. General Assembly scheduled to begin September 20. However, he cancelled his trip, claiming that the United States could not guarantee his safety within its borders because of the animosity arising out of the Korean jetliner incident. At a meeting of the U.N.'s Committee on Relations with the Host Country, the Soviet delegate, Igor Yakovlev, charged that the United States had grossly flouted the host-country agreement with the U.N. in failing to provide the proper security for Gromyko.

In an emotional response, the American deputy delegate, Charles Lichenstein, said that the Soviet Ambassador's accusation was a palpable falsehood.

> If in a judicious determination of the members of the United Nations, they feel they are not welcome and they are not being treated with the hostly consideration that is their due, then the United States strongly encourages such member states seriously to consider removing themselves and this organization from the soil of the United States.
>
> We will put no impediment in your way. The members of the U.S. mission to the United Nations will be down at the dockside waving you fond farewell as you sail into the sunset.

Lichenstein was pointing out that the Americans had taken so much abuse from the Third World nations and from the Soviet Union that they were fed up with the crap they were getting from the United Nations crowd.

What the U.S. really had in mind was that the United Nations should now think seriously about spending half its time in its headquarters in New York and half its time in other headquarters – in Moscow. If they had to sit in Moscow for six months of the year, the naive anti-American and anti-capitalist members of the United Nations might finally realize some of the benefits of living in a free society, which offered a cornucopia of consumer goods along with a high living standard.

The United States' proposal to split the hosting between

the U.S.A. and the U.S.S.R. has the support of President Reagan and will probably be vigorously pursued.

It may well be one of the few good things in the fallout from the 747 massacre.

14

THE WINNER OF THE
PROPAGANDA WAR

THERE WERE other factors that had influenced China and certain Third World nations in the Security Council to abstain in the belief that the 747's destruction "had been clouded with too much uncertainty."

Another disconcerting event had occurred on September 9, just three days before the vote. It was what the *New York Times* called a "spellbinding performance in Moscow" by the Soviet Chief of Staff, Marshal Nikolai V. Ogarkov, when he appeared at an unprecedented press conference before the western world's and the Soviet's media.

He was the top soldier of the Soviet Union, second only in the hierarchy to Marshal Ustinov, the Minister of Defense in the Politburo.

Marshal Ogarkov was flanked at the press conference by Georgi Korniyenko, a First Deputy Foreign Minister, and Leonid Zamyatin, head of the Central Committee's Information Department and a veteran propagandist. The fact that all three were there and prepared to submit to intensive questioning certified the depth of the Soviet government's concern about the 747 incident and its potential impact on the international image of the Soviet Union.

In essence, Ogarkov's case followed the same line that had been established in government statements made through TASS:

- the Korean 747 was equipped with advanced inertial navigation equipment and was guided by extensive ground-control installations, so could not inadvertently stray as far off course as it had;

- the aircraft did not acknowledge the radio and visual signals from the Soviet interceptors;
- the aircraft flew over some of the Soviet Union's most sensitive nuclear missile bases;
- the aircraft emitted bursts of radio transmissions that were tied to its espionage role;
- U.S. and Japanese air traffic and military controllers could have warned it that it was off course and that it was being followed, but remained silent;
- the 747 had rendezvoused with the RC-135 that controlled it;
- the Korean aircraft was flying without lights;
- the aircraft had sharply altered its course to approach the Soviet Air Defense Forces base on Sakhalin. "There was no doubt then that . . . it was a reconnaissance plane," according to Ogarkov.

This press conference demonstrated that, even though Ogarkov made statements of "fact" that were contradicted by the evidence on the Su-15 pilot's tape – for example, that "the Soviet pilot didn't see the lights" of the 747, when the tapes clearly demonstrated that he had seen the navigation and beacon lights – the Soviets could still offer a strong, credible justification for their actions and the decision to destroy the intruder aircraft.

Ogarkov, with all the weight of his position, was there to explain what had happened *as the Soviet Union saw it*. Yes, there might be inconsistencies as to some of the facts but, in the over-all scheme of things, the Soviets had had no choice but to recognize the intruder as a reconnaissance aircraft. They had had no choice but to shoot it down.

And who was really to blame? The United States, of course, because the espionage mission was being conducted for and controlled by the United States. There were many approving nods in the press conference when Ogarkov said, "Let me say that in this case, a fairly old and primitive method is being applied: the outcry that the guilty person raises in order to divert suspicion from his own person." The United States, the "guilty person", was raising the outcry.

Ogarkov's "spellbinding performance" was the cornerstone of the entire Soviet propaganda and counter-propaganda strategy against the United States. It was to pay enormous credibility dividends in the United States and throughout the free world. And it had a powerful influence on the wavering members of the U.N. Security Council during the next three days, as they considered whether they should vote for or against the resolution condemning the Soviet Union, or should abstain from voting entirely.

The major barrages in the propaganda war had now been fired: the Reagan and Shultz statements and speeches; the Soviet government's TASS statements; Kirkpatrick's strong speech at the United Nations; and, finally, Ogarkov's press conference.

The lines were drawn. The differences between both sides had been established; the retaliation steps had been taken.

Now the Soviet and American governments and their representatives would carry on with their accusatory rhetoric at the United Nations, at disarmament conferences and in speeches and press releases whenever the opportunity arose.

Like all other monumental issues and confrontations, save those that cause a war, the shouting match between the American Eagle and the Russian Bear over the 747 massacre gradually began to subside.

But although the furor has died down somewhat, the 747 massacre remains an issue in the minds of the public, both because of the many unanswered questions that remain and because almost everyone has an opinion about what happened: about whether the aircraft was indeed on a spying mission; about whether the Soviet fighter pilot could in fact see that the aircraft was a 747 civilian airliner; about whether the Soviets were justified in shooting the aircraft down; and about countless other troublesome questions.

The astonishing effectiveness of the Soviet counter-propaganda campaign was clearly demonstrated by a *New York Times*/CBS *News* poll published on September 16, a week after the Ogarkov press conference had been broadcast throughout America, and just five days after the U.S. changing of the Soviet fighter pilot's tapes.

The *New York Times*/CBS *News* poll was based on telephone interviews conducted on September 14 with 705 adults selected from around the United States, excluding Alaska and Hawaii. The question put was: "Do you think the American Government has told the public all they know about this incident, or is the Government in Washington holding back information that people ought to know?"

An astonishing 61 per cent believed the government was holding back, 23 per cent thought it had told all and 16 per cent didn't know.

Furthermore, skepticism pervaded all groups: 62 per cent of the men in the sample group were skeptical while 25 per cent were not; 61 per cent of the women were skeptical, while 22 per cent were not.

The *New York Times* reported that many among those who believed the government was holding back "feel that the presence of an intelligence plane near Soviet airspace two hours before the attack on the airliner meant the United States 'bears a significant share of the blame for the incident'."

The evidence of "a tape recording of a Soviet pilot . . . talking of firing a cannon when an earlier transcription had no such comment" had also influenced the skeptics.

Strangely enough, if the Reagan Administration had in fact "held back" the information about the RC-135, the Soviets, who knew nothing about its being in the area until the President told them, would not have been able to use it as a support for their electronic espionage allegation. The American public would not have known about it and it therefore could not have caused 61 per cent of those polled to believe that the government was holding back.

From the date of that poll to the time of writing, there have been few, if any, new factors disclosed that would change the mind of the American public or, for that matter, of the rest of the western world. We must conclude, then, that, hands down, the Soviets won the war of propaganda and counter-propaganda in the United States of America.

Of course, there is never any question about who will win in the Soviet Union. There is simply no contest, because of the complete control that the government has over the news media and the release of information to the Soviet people.

The Soviets waged a masterful word-war, and won a classic rhetoric victory over the United States. It was one of the most successful disinformation and propaganda achievements in modern times.

15

ISSUES UNRESOLVED

WHEN THE main shouting match was over between the
United States and the Soviet Union, there were several major
fundamental disagreements left on the table between
them.

Each nation was satisfied that the other was lying. That
difference will never be resolved. It is rooted in the
irreconcilable ideological conflicts and the various historical
factors that make the two nations totally incapable of
understanding and trusting each other – in the fundamental
differences between communist dictatorship and western
capitalist democracy.

The principal points of controversy and disagreement
between them include the following:

- *The purpose of the flight.* The United States maintained
  that Flight 007 was simply a commercial scheduled flight
  that inadvertently went off course; the Soviets claimed
  that it was on an electronic intelligence "spy" mission
  over hypersensitive areas of the Kamchatka Peninsula
  and Sakhalin Island, and that the 747 was being directed
  by a U.S. RC-135 reconnaissance aircraft to overfly a
  Soviet area where a most important base for the strategic
  nuclear forces of the U.S.S.R. was located;
- *The weather conditions*: President Reagan claimed that
  the destruction of the 747 occurred on a "clear night with
  a half-moon," while the Soviets countered by saying that
  it happened in conditions of bad visibility. The ICAO
  report said: "the moon was in the last quarter with

approximately 45 per cent of the disc illuminated. At 18:00 hours, the moon was about 60 degrees above the horizon" and "cloud coverage increased approaching southern Sakhalin to a condition of mostly overcast low cloud with scattered medium and high clouds, the latter in streaks . . . ." This meant that at 35,000 feet, as was clear from the tapes, pilot 805 could see the "target" without any difficulty;

The navigational lights: The Soviet line, and that taken by Marshal Ogarkov, was that the 747 displayed no navigational or strobe lights; the U.S. claim was that the aircraft was equipped with standard navigational lighting – that is, strobe, fuselage and wing lights – and that they were illuminated. The taped transmissions of the Soviet fighter pilot bear this out. On the other hand the ICAO report says that Flight 007 was not equipped with strobe anti-collision lights, but had red anti-collision rotating beacons and that they and the navigational lights were on when the aircraft left Anchorage. The ICAO report says: the "KAL logo light on the vertical fin was normally illuminated, but its use was at the discretion of the pilot-in-command. It was common practice for many airlines, including KAL, to fly at night with window curtains lowered." It follows that, if the aircraft's navigation lights were on and its red anti-collison rotating beacons were flashing (as was clearly the case when the Soviet pilot said he could see the lights), it is possible that the KAL logo light on the vertical fin was also illuminated. In that event, the Soviet pilot would have been able to see not only the aircraft, but also the KAL insignia on its tail;

Radio contact. The Soviets claim that attempts were made by Soviet pilots to establish radio contact through universal emergency channel 121.5 megacycles, but that these efforts were ignored; the Americans claimed that the Soviet military aircraft radios were not equipped with that channel because among other things the availability of that frequency might assist defecting Soviet pilots. On the other hand, retired U.S. Air Force Chief of Intelligence, Major-General George J. Keegan, Jr., said that he had personal knowledge that the Su-15 was in fact equipped with the 121.5 frequency, However, even if this were true, the Soviet fighter pilot would have had to communicate with the Korean aircraft in the universal language of the air – English – a language which apparently he did not speak; furthermore, there was no record in 805's transmissions to his ground station that he had attempted to communicate on 121.5, unless the transmission at 18:13:26 can be so interpreted – the ICAO translation is "the target isn't responding to the call," whereas the official U.S. version is "the target isn't responding to I.F.F. (Identification/Friend or Foe);"

– *The spying issue.* The Soviets claim, because of the alleged rendezvous of the 747 with the RC-135, and other factors, that they were led to believe that the 747 was in fact an American electronic espionage aircraft which did not respond to ICAO interception signals, and that they were therefore justified in shooting it down; since the aircraft was on a U.S. reconnaissance mission, the Americans were to blame. The Americans denied all such allegations, claiming that the aircraft was simply a civilian airliner and that the Soviet Union had no justification whatsoever for shooting it down. As President Reagan pointed out, the United States does not shoot down foreign aircraft over American territory, even though Aeroflot and Cuban commercial airliners have overflown "sensitive U.S. military facilities."

It should be noted that the conclusions of the ICAO report deal very gingerly with the the Soviets' justification of their actions. No blame is levelled at the Soviet Union, with the following mild exception:

> k) the U.S.S.R. authorities assumed that KE 007 was an intelligence aircraft and, therefore, did not make

exhaustive efforts to identify the aircraft through inflight visual observation.

The ICAO report contributes little to the resolution of the main points of disagreement between the Americans and the Soviets. The one thing it is careful not to do is to allocate blame.

The other thing it is careful not to do is to attribute a cause other than pilot error for Flight 007's being off course and in the place it was when it was shot down.

When the search for the black boxes and the fuselage of the KAL 747 was abandoned early in November, the opportunity was forever lost to find the information that might provide the answers to many contentious questions. Was there electronic espionage gear on the aircraft? Were the pilots aware they were being intercepted by the Soviet fighters? Did they know where they were? Was there any attempt by the Soviet fighter pilots or ground stations to reach them on International Emergency Channel 121.5 megacycles?

The answers lie at the bottom of the Sea of Japan. They also lie in some of the logical deductions that can be made from the facts that are known.

16

WHO GAVE THE ORDER
TO SHOOT?

WHO WAS IT in the Soviet political or military hierarchy who made the decision to "stop the flight" of the intruder aircraft?

The answer to this question will never be disclosed by the Soviets, who are anxious to maintain secrecy in order to protect the senior members of their hierarchies.

On the other hand, analysis of what has been said, particularly by Marshal Ogarkov at his September 9 press conference, permits us to place the responsibility first at a particular level, then with one person.

Since 1980 the position of the Air Defense Forces has changed in relation to the over-all Soviet command structure. Up to that time, the commanders of the ADF districts and regions reported directly to the Commander-in-Chief of National Air Defense, Marshal A. I. Koldunov at his central command post at Kalinin some fifty kilometers northwest of Moscow. Koldunov was subordinate only to Marshal Ogarkov, the Soviet Chief of General Staff and Deputy Minister of Defense. Ogarkov in turn was subordinate to Marshal Ustinov, the Minister of Defense and a senior member of the Politburo.

The recent changes in the command structure removed the district Air Defense Force commanders from the direct control of ADF headquarters in Moscow and placed them under the control of the theatre commander of their geographic area. As a result, the ADF general in command of the Biya region and responsible for the air defense of the Kamchatka and Sakhalin area came under the control of the commander of the Soviet Far East region who, at the time of the 747 event, was General Vladimir Govorov, a fifty-eight-year-old member of the Communist Party Central Committee.

Therefore, the chain of command on the night of August 31-September 1, 1983, was: ADF commander of the Biya region, to commander Far East Region, to Commander-in-Chief of National Air Defense, Marshal Koldunov at the Air Defense Forces Headquarters in Moscow (because it was an air matter), to Marshal Ogarkov, military Chief of General Staff. In the chain, the Far East region commander might have gone direct to Ogarkov, or at least kept Orgarkov's headquarters in Moscow informed, while also communicating with Koldunov.

If Ogarkov needed direction he would go then to Marshal Ustinov, the Defense Minister who, as a member of the Politburo, wore two hats, one political, the other military.

The time frame for the commanders in Moscow, during the more than two hours the Korean 747 was transiting Soviet airspace and the Sea of Okhotsk, was, as Marshal Ogarkov put it in his press conference, from shortly after 4 a.m. to 6:24 a.m. of September 1, local Sakhalin time, or from shortly after 8:00 p.m. to 10:24 p.m. on the evening of August 31, Moscow time. This, of course, is the dinner or post-dinner period for commanders-in-chief and their senior staff – a time when the vodka level is high, in true Russian tradition.

OUT IN THE real, harsh world of the Soviet Far East region, an event was taking shape. As reported by special correspondent Boris Reznik, in the Moscow newspaper, *Izvestiya*, in its morning edition of September 12,

> . . . the radar scanners at the Air Defense Forces sub-unit tracking station here on the desolate, rocky coast of Kamchatka seem to be filled with the biting winds which blow constantly from the Pacific. Good weather is a

rarity in these parts, with their storms, fog and thick cloud. Officer Oleg Pakhomov's team was on combat watch that night. The tense silence of the control centre was broken by operator Pvt. Sergey Osipov's voice: "Target spotted." The tracks of an unidentified aircraft crept across the radar installation's flickering screen.

So the event began that was to see the Soviet Air Defense Forces planes fail to intercept the intruder over Kamchatka – although the Soviets were later to claim that they had. It was a failure that would put great pressure on the ADF district commander at Biya to carry out the responsibilities laid on him by the Seventh Session of the Tenth U.S.S.R. Supreme Soviet in 1982 when it adopted Article 36, whereby, for ADF aircraft carrying out the defense of the U.S.S.R.'s frontiers: "in cases where an end to a violation or the apprehension of violators cannot be achieved by other means, weapons must be used."

As the pressure of the failure to halt the "spy plane" increased, a decision had to be made. As Marshal Ogarkov put it in his press conference; "It's absolutely evident it wasn't a plane that simply lost its way, but . . . an aircraft sent on a special mission . . . We had dragged on our activities for two hours and a half and were totally convinced that we were dealing with a reconnaissance airplane that was totally ignoring all signals from our control forces. What was left to us?"

What was left was the decision to destroy the intruder.

We can deduce who made the decision from the answers Ogarkov himself gave at the press conference.

It is important to understand that, in Soviet military jargon, a "command post" includes higher headquarters, not only in the field but in Moscow as well. The ADF headquarters in Kalinin near Moscow is its "central command post." The Air Defense Forces general commanding the Biya district occupied the district command post, and under him there was a "command post" for each zone of his region. Furthermore, the headquarters of General Ogarkov in Moscow and of the commander of the Far East region were also "command posts."

Starting at the bottom of the chain of command it is perfectly clear and accepted that the pilot of the Su-15 did not report the identity of the target aircraft because it was not his duty to do so; it was also not his duty to make the decision to destroy it. As he later said in his television interview, "but he [the 747] continued to fly on the same course, at the same height, and I received an order, a precise and definite order." It was an order from the ground to destroy the target. He executed the order.

At the September 9 press conference, Marshal Ogarkov had to deal with a series of questions. His answers are illuminating.

His terse response to the question, "Who gave the order to cut the flight short?" is deceptively simple:

> A. "The order to the pilots was given by the commander of the Biya region."

This was confirmed by Ogarkov in his answer to a following question which was put to him on the decision to terminate the flight made by the district commander: "Am I to take it that that means there was no consultation with anybody in Moscow . . . ?"

> A. "There is a strict order of command and responsibility and action in such situations in the Soviet Union. How the decision was made, I already told you. The decision was made by the district commander."

That is a far more direct statement than the previous one. But in the light of the several errors and pieces of disinformation produced by Ogarkov that day – "the Soviet pilot didn't see the light;" the RC-135 rendezvoused with the 747; there was a change of course at Sakhalin – the attribution by Ogarkov to the Biya commander is highly suspect. This is particularly so because it was in Ogarkov's personal interest to distance the decision-making as far down from his own position as he could, particularly if it was he himself who had in fact made the decision to destroy the 747.

Some analysts think that the Biya commander made the decision and gave the order without referring the matter to the Far East region commander or to Moscow because to do so would show him to be indecisive and not capable of command and control.

On the other hand, a tight command and control structure is maintained in the Soviet military. The demands of this structure would require the Biya regional commander to inform the commander of the Far East region at Khabarovsk. At the same time, the Biya general would inform the Air Defense Forces Central Command Post at Kalinin, and Marshal Koldunov as soon as he had received information from the Kamchatka radar sub-unit that an intruder had entered the sixty-mile line beyond the "border." It is impossible to believe that it would not be mandatory for this important intelligence to be passed straight up both to Koldunov's and to Ogarkov's command posts.

Once that was done it would be necessary to keep passing progress or status reports up the same chain. That this passage of information took place is made perfectly clear by Ogarkov.

The following excerpts from Marshal Ogarkov's answers demonstrate unequivocally that all "command posts," including his own and that of the Air Defense Force in Moscow, were fully informed of the event as it was happening:

> All our defense systems, which for two and a half hours took action to force it to land, as of the beginning of the flight, *at all command posts*, were completely sure what we were dealing with here was a reconnaissance plane.

And let me add that all command levels – we reached the total conviction that we were dealing with a reconnaissance plane and we were trying to force it to land in Kamchatka. But when it did not react to 120 warning shots, nothing was left to us but [to] act the way we did.

Termination of that flight – of the flight of the intruder ... aircraft – was not error. Antiaircraft defense forces attempted to stop ... to force it to land using all the capabilities possible and at *all command posts* of our system complete conviction was achieved we were dealing with a reconnoitering plane.

In these statements there is a clear admission that all command posts in the Soviet system, including Ogarkov's own command post, knew what was going on, and were involved in the process as it was happening.

Ogarkov's use of the word "we" is also significant: "... we reached the total conviction that we were dealing with a reconnaissance plane and we were trying to force it to land in Kamchatka."

It is almost impossible to believe that the all-powerful Ogarkov, having been apprised of a situation and having watched it develop over a two-hour period, would not himself have given the order to destroy the aircraft or, alternatively, have endorsed a request from the commander at Biya to destroy the intruder. One way or the other, Marshal Ogarkov's admissions at his press conference point directly to him as the person who made or approved the decision to terminate the flight.

His answer to the question about the role of the political and military hierarchy in Moscow further confirmed his direct involvement. He replied by saying: "There is probably no general staff in the world which in such a situation would not receive reports of such an incident."

There is one final piece of evidence that implicates

Ogarkov as the man who made the decision. It is that the Chief of General Staff himself would appear at a press conference before the media of the western world to justify the action of the Soviet military in shooting down the KAL 747 and killing 269 civilians. Such an action was unprecedented. For Ogarkov, a man dedicated to secrecy and a low profile, to take this unusual step meant that he must have had a powerful personal motive. There might have been some direction from Ustinov or the Politburo for him to meet the press, but it is far more likely that Ogarkov himself decided to go public and obtained Ustinov's – and also, perhaps, the sickly Andropov's – approval.

Because it was absolutely essential that he should cover his own tracks, he could not leave the public relations exercise to anyone else – certainly not to the commander at Biya. The facts as Ogarkov saw them and wanted to present them had to be without flaw; if there were weaknesses in the case, only his presence and authority could carry the situation.

Did he do his job well? To repeat what the *New York Times* said, he put on a "spellbinding performance."

On October 4, 1983, the news from Moscow was that several senior Soviet officers had been removed from their jobs in the Far East military command as a result of the apparent inefficiency of the Air Defense Forces in the shooting down of the Korean 747. Evidently Marshal Ogarkov decided it was necessary to take other highly visible steps to distance the responsibility for the 747 massacre from himself and the Politburo.

17

THE ICAO REPORT

ON DECEMBER 13, 1983, the International Civil Aviation Organization made public the final report of the investigation team assigned to determine the facts and technical aspects relating to the flight and destruction of Korean Air Lines Flight 007.

On March 1, 1984, the ICAO Council met in Montreal to consider the report. Nothing had changed. The U.S. wanted to censure the U.S.S.R. In turn, the Soviets continued their claim that Flight 007 was on a spy mission for the U.S. On March 6 the U.S. censure motion was passed.

The team had made visits to Japan, the Republic of Korea and the United States, and to the Sea of Japan. In addition, the Secretary General of ICAO, Yves Lambert, had been in the Union of Soviet Socialist Republics at the invitation of its Minister of Civil Aviation. He had been accompanied by the leader of the ICAO investigation team. In the U.S.S.R. the two men met with the Minister of Civil Aviation and had two meetings with the Accident Investigation Commission of the U.S.S.R. They visited a military air base where they saw an Su-15 interceptor similar to the one used on September 1, 1983. The capability of this aircraft to communicate on the 121.5 frequency was demonstrated during the visit.

From November 16 to 18, 1983, two members of the investigation team with the Director of the Air Navigation Bureau of ICAO directed several flight simulations at the Boeing Company's installations at Seattle. The purpose of the simulations was to explore various scenarios the investigation team had developed as possible explanations for the straying of Flight 007. Also participating in the simulation effort were officials from the Republic of Korea, Korean Air Lines, the Boeing Aircraft Company, Litton Aero Products Inc. (the manufacturer of the INS system on board Flight 007), and the United States Federal Aviation Administration, which certifies both the Boeing 747 and the Litton INS systems.

In addition to the simulations, which were conducted using a Boeing Company flight-training simulator, an exploratory engineering simulation was conducted for the investigation by CAE Electronics Limited of Montreal. Discussions leading up to the simulations were conducted with Air Canada experts as well as with Litton Systems Canada Ltd. of Toronto.

Given that this report is made by an investigation team composed of experienced members of an international industry anxious to avoid giving itself a bad name, and intent on distancing the industry from the responsibility for the event and on avoiding making accusations against the crew of Flight 007 or the nations that were party to the incident, it would be expected that the report would be inconclusive on the major questions. The report measures up fully to that expectation.

On the question whether the crew of Flight 007 knew where they were when their flight was terminated by the Su-15, the investigation team really came to no conclusion at all except that "no evidence was found . . . to indicate that the flight crew of KE 007 was, at any time, aware of the flight's deviation from its planned route in spite of the fact that it continued along the same general off-track flight path for some five hours and twenty-six minutes." This "conclusion" is found on page 55 of the report. However, on the previous page, the investigation team made it perfectly clear that the KAL crew knew or ought to have known where they were. The investigation team admitted it had had difficulty in understanding the causes of the five hour and twenty-six minute divergence from the flight-planned route, saying that its difficulty was due to three factors.

The first factor was that "the flight did not adjust its outbound track to cross Bethel VOR." That is, the captain of Flight 007 failed to take the easy procedure of following the outbound track from Anchorage to cross Bethel VOR. With the sophisticated navigational gear on board, this failure was clear evidence that he fully intended to take the aircraft past Bethel twelve nautical miles to the north. The aircraft's gradual deviation to the north of its assigned route began only ten minutes after its departure from Anchorage. It is impossible to believe that the deviation was unintentional.

The second factor which the investigation team had difficulty in understanding, they put this way: "If the navigation aids at St. Paul Island and Shemya were not received, this discordancy should have caused the crew to recheck and validate its navigational progress." This means that the 747 was out of range of the navigation aids early in the flight, at St. Paul Island and Shemya, just as it was out of range of VHF communications with Anchorage. This should have caused the crew to recheck and validate their navigational progress, when they would have found out that they were well off course. This highly experienced crew, so well-trained and qualified, had flown this route many times before. It is impossible to believe that they would not have rechecked and validated their position – unless they knew where they were and intended to be there.

The final factor that caused the investigation team difficulty was that "the weather radar could have been used in the ground-mapping mode as a means of cross-checking position or to serve as an alert to navigational problems." The report notes that the aircraft was equipped with two Bendix RDR-IF weather radar sets and the associated wave guide and aerial system. The radar had a maximum range of 200 NM with a 180-degree scan capability. This means it could "see" straight ahead through 90 degrees to the left and to the right of the aircraft. After noting that the weather radar was serviceable, the ICAO report states:

It is common practice – especially at night – in all over-ocean areas and near coastlines, for pilots of aircraft equipped with airborne radar, to observe landfalls and to assess their navigational accuracy by means of the ground mapping capability of such equipment. Nearby to the left and to the right of route R20, well within the range of airborne weather radar of the type carried on KE 007, are located Shemya, the Komandorskiye Islands, the Kamchatka Peninsula and the Kuril Islands, which were readily discernible topography. Use of the radar on this route, required by some airlines, was a common practice in Korean Air Lines. Its use should have provided an early indication to the pilot of KE 007 that the flight was straying to the right of route R20. It can only be concluded that the radar system either was not functioning properly or that it was not used. Had the radar not been functioning properly it should have caused the pilot to seek alternative opportunities to cross-check and verify the accuracy of his navigation. There were no indications that such actions were taken.

To repeat, there were two radar systems on board the air-craft, which means that if one had become unserviceable, the other would still be functioning. There was one other con-clusion about the weather radar system that the investigation team studiously avoided, although it is the conclusion that is most probable. It is that the radar was functioning properly, that it was being used in the mapping mode as was "a common practice in Korean Air Lines" and that through use of the weather radar, as he approached and overflew the Kamchatka Peninsula and as he approached and overflew Sakhalin Island, the captain knew exactly where he was.

Shortly after the Flight 007 events, Captain Kim Chang Kyu, the pilot of the KAL Boeing 707 that was shot down by the Soviets in 1978, said that once an aircraft approaches the Russian and Japanese islands, they can be easily seen on the aircraft's weather radar in the mapping mode and that "everybody uses weather radar in that area along route R20."

Notwithstanding its own difficulty in understanding the causes and duration of the divergence of Flight 007, the investigation team ignored its difficulties and the factors behind them in order to conclude that "no evidence was found. . .to indicate that the flight crew of KE 007 was, at any time, aware of the flight's deviation from its planned route . . . ."

Another element in the mix of difficulties faced by the investigation team was the record of excellence of the pilot-in-command, Chun Byung In. They noted that his total flying experience was 10,627 hours. His time on the Boeing 747 was 6,618 hours. His experience on the North Pacific (NORPAC) composite routes was eighty-three flights between February 4, 1973, and August 27, 1983. He had flown twenty-seven times on route R20 since February 1, 1979. In the twelve months before the incident, he had flown the route twice, both times within the previous three months. His most recent flight on route R20 from Anchorage to Seoul was on August 16, 1983.

The following statement made by the investigating team must have caused them enormous difficulty when trying to reconcile what it says against the conclusion that the captain was not aware of the flight's deviation from its planned route:

> He passed instrument and proficiency checks on the B747 on 3 and 4 April 1983 (simulator and aircraft) and on 22 July 1983 completed a route check on the Anchorage-Tokyo (Narita)-Seoul route (over-all grading – excellent; on INS pre-flight and cruise procedures – excellent). In a further route check on 12-14 July 1983 on the route Bangkok-Bahrain-Jeddah, the following comments were recorded: "He follows the regulations and specifications and has a good knowledge of INS operational procedures."

Could this man not have known for five hours and twenty-six minutes that his aircraft had deviated badly from its planned route? And could his highly experienced co-pilot, Sohn Dong Hui, with 3,441 hours on the B747 also have been unaware?

The investigators carried out a simulation of several navigational-error scenarios and intentional deviations from the assigned track R20. As stated in their report, in the scenarios tested, due consideration was given to aspects which would have affected the flight path of Flight 007. These included magnetic variation, upper winds and aircraft conditions. The simulations and calculations covered the following possibilities:

1) Great Circle track from 12 NM north of Bethel to Seoul.
2) Great Circle track from R20 through the approximate last-known position to Seoul.
3) Maintaining a constant magnetic heading of 240 degrees from a position 12 NM north of Bethel.
4) The simulated following on a constant magnetic heading of 246 degrees from the time the aircraft was cleared to proceed on its own mode of navigation.
5) A simulation of the results of an erroneous insertion of the present (ramp) position (10 degrees too far east) into all three Inertial Navigation Systems.
6) Insertion of the present (ramp) position (10 degrees too far east) into the controlling Inertial Navigation System only.

After rather elaborate explanations as to the conduct and findings of each of the simulations, all but scenarios 4) and 6) were abandoned.

Using prudent, cautious language, the investigation team tentatively concluded:

> In the absence of the flight data recorder and the cockpit voice recorder there was insufficient information to draw firm conclusions; it was possible to postulate that

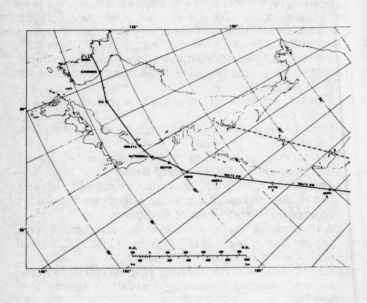

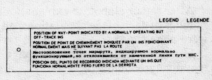
Map 17:1   ICAO map of KE 007 possible track if pilot error: ICAO scenarios 5 and 6.

CHART   CARTE   КАРТА   CARTA   6

COMPARATIVE TRACK AND WAY-POINT PASSAGE POSITIONS FOR SCENARIO No. 5 & 6
COMPARAISON DES ROUTES ET DES POSITIONS AU PASSAGE DES POINTS DE CHEMINEMENT SELON LE SCENARIO No. 5 & 6
ДАННЫЕ О МЕСТОПОЛОЖЕНИИ НА ЛИНИИ ПУТИ И ПО ПРОХОЖДЕНИИ ТОЧЕК МАРШРУТА ДЛЯ СЦЕНАРИЯ № 5 & 6
COMPARACION DE LA DERROTA Y POSICIONES AL PASAR POR LOS PUNTOS DE RECORRIDO EN EL CASO DE LA HIPOTESIS Num. 5 & 6

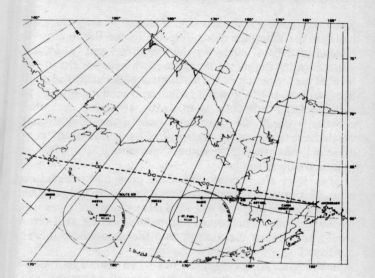

ЛЕГЕНДА   CLAVE

POSITION OF WAY-POINT INDICATED BY AN INS WITH A 10° EASTERLY
ERROR IN THE INITIAL POSITION
POSTION DE POINT DE CHEMINEMENT INDIQUEE PAR UN INS AFFECTE
D'UNE ERREUR DE POSITION INITIALE DE 10° VERS L'EST
Местоположение точек маршрута, индицируемое ИНС с
ошибкой в 10° к востоку в исходном положении.
POSICION DEL PUNTO DE RECORRIDO INDICADA POR UN INS CON ERROR
DE 10° HACIA EL ESTE DE LA POSICION INICIAL

either the holding of a constant magnetic heading (246 degrees) or an undetected error of 10 degrees east in longitude made in the insertion of the present (ramp) position into one of the three INS units would have produced a track to the area of KE 007's destruction that is also consistent with radar track information provided by the USSR and by Japan.

The investigating team was saying that, if in error the crew had left the autopilot mode selector in the heading mode instead of the INS mode for the five hours and twenty-six minutes of the flight (the autopilot mode selector sits at eye level at the top center of the instrument panel at arm's length between both pilots, and is a switch of crucial importance to which regular reference is made by sweeping eyes that constantly check the instrument panel), then the aircraft would have flown itself to the south of Sakhalin Island "very close in time to that of the actual flight though 80 to 100 NM (nautical miles) south."

They were also saying that if the crew had inserted an erroneous present (ramp) position co-ordinate in longitude into only one of the three INS units when the aircraft was still on the ground at Anchorage and before moving, that error would have taken the aircraft into the area where it was destroyed.

In reference to accuracy checks when the waypoint co-ordinates are being punched into the INS systems, the investigation team noted:

In the aircraft, the KAL procedure was for the co-pilot to switch on the three Inertial Navigation Systems, insert the present (ramp) position, confirmed from the Route Manual, and initiate system alignment. The KAL procedures required each flight crew member to check the present (ramp) position entry. Waypoint co-ordinates would then be entered during the system alignment.

If these procedures were followed for the start-up of Flight 007 at Anchorage, all three of the flight crew members would have checked the present (ramp) position. There could have been no 10-degree error as postulated by the ICAO team.

As the investigation team admits in its final conclusion, which deals with both of the above propositions, "Each of those postulations assumed a considerable degree of lack of alertness and attentiveness on the part of the entire flight crew but not to a degree that was unknown in international civil aviation."

It is noted that there is absolutely no evidence whatsoever in the report to justify the you-know-how-it-is words "but not to a degree that was unknown in international civil aviation." The facts simply cannot be swept away by such a gratuitous statement. There was no evidence at all of lack of alertness or attentiveness. The pilots were certainly attentive and alert when they were passing their erroneous waypoint checks through Flight 015 and by HF radio when they were well out of VHF range and knew they ought not to have been.

On the basis of the evidence contained in the ICAO report, and weighing all of the known factors about Flight 007, it is not possible to believe that the crew of the aircraft did not know where they were and had not programmed one INS to fly the direct Anchorage-Seoul route, while the other was to receive and monitor the waypoints so they could be reported en route.

18

WHY FLIGHT 007 WAS
OVER SAKHALIN

THE FINAL QUESTION to be dealt with is: Why did Captain
Chun take his aircraft along or near the Great Circle Route
from Anchorage to Seoul when he knew that he would have
to cross highly sensitive Soviet airspace for well over two
hours?

Was Flight 007 on a spying mission? From the moment the
Soviet government issued its first defensive statement on
September 1 the allegation was that the Korean 747 was on a
spying mission for the American Central Intelligence
Agency. More than anything else, this charge raised
suspicion in the minds of the American public and of people
throughout the western world. The fact was that the Soviet
Air Defense Forces radar personnel who picked up the blip
of the intruder on the morning of September 1 as it approached the Kamchatka Peninsula were convinced that the
intruder was a spy aircraft. As related previously, there is no
indication that, at the time, they had any knowledge that the
RC-135 was in proximity to the on-coming intruder. It was
simply that they believed that the huge aircraft heading
toward their sensitive airspace could be there for only one
reason – electronic espionage. So far as the Soviets were
concerned, it then followed that they were entitled to
intercept the aircraft and, if necessary, destroy it. Furthermore since those on the ground were convinced that it
was an intelligence aircraft, there was no need for the
interceptor pilot who eventually found it to identify it.

Indeed that was the explanation accepted by the ICAO investigation team when they said in their conclusion (k) that the Soviet authorities assumed that Flight 007 was an intelligence aircraft, and therefore did not make exhaustive efforts to identify the aircraft through in-flight visual observations. As the tapes show, the Su-15 pilot passed no identification information to the ground, although he saw the aircraft and knew what it was. He said several times that he saw the lights of the aircraft, which might have included the KAL logo light on the vertical fin. According to the ICAO report, that light "was normally illuminated but its use was at the discretion of the pilot-in-command."

There were two compartments to the Soviet espionage charges.

The first was described and dealt with in the ICAO report as follows:

It was stated in the USSR preliminary investigation report that the flight was involved in a mission co-ordinated with other agencies, to test the air defense system of the USSR. The departure time from Anchorage was stated to have been delayed by forty minutes to coincide with certain satellite orbital positions or passages. This was viewed in light of the standard Korean Air Lines practice of separately calculating the ETD (estimated time of departure) for each flight of KE 007 so as to result in an on-time arrival at Seoul at 0600 (local time).

Not only was 6:00 hours (local) at Seoul the scheduled arrival time, but also passenger handling and customs services were not available prior to that time. On the other hand, the control tower would be open and Flight 007 would be able to land at twenty-seven minutes to six if Captain Chun chose to do so. He then could have taxied up to his normal gate and shut down, keeping his passengers on board until the handling and customs services were available.

The ICAO report explains why the scheduled departure

from Anchorage at 12:20 hours GMT (3:20 local time) was changed.

> The scheduled block-to-block time for Anchorage-Seoul was eight hours twenty minutes with a scheduled time of arrival (at Seoul) of 2100 hours (0600 Korean standard time). Due to less head wind than the average prevailing winds, the flight time on the computer flight plan was seven hours fifty-three minutes. Accordingly the departure from the gate at Anchorage was re-scheduled to 1250 hours, and the aircraft was airborne at 1300 hours GMT (0400 local).

For these reasons the ICAO investigation team concluded that "there is no supporting evidence that the departure time of KE 007 was planned for any other purpose or to accommodate an intelligence mission."

The Soviets' second espionage charge had to do with photography and the use of cameras on board the 747 to photograph secret installations. The difficulty with this argument is that the advanced U.S. satellite, the KH11, sends images to earth electronically from its altitude of one hundred miles or more. Those photographs, after magnification, have been known to show the bolt on the deck of a Soviet cruiser or a man on the street reading *Pravda* with the name of the paper clearly visible in the photograph. What would be gained by sending a civilian airliner to take photographs, when the job was already being done by satellite or, for that matter, by the SR-71 Blackbird, the American supersonic strategic reconnaissance aircraft, which can operate at ceilings of more than eighty thousand feet?

A jet aircraft that has vertical cameras on board will have bulges in its belly to accommodate the cameras and the glass plates through which the cameras take their pictures. Modifications of this kind are readily discernible to mainten-ance people servicing such aircraft wherever they may be in the world. According to Korean Air Lines officials, no camera equipment was onboard Flight 007, and neither it nor any of its sister aircraft are equipped with cameras.

On the other hand Aeroflot, LOT Polish Air Lines and CSA, the Czechoslovak airline, as well as the Cuban air carrier, are notorious in the airline industry for their photographic intelligence "mistakes" in wandering off their assigned routes and photographing sensitive U.S., Canadian and other military facilities.

During 1981-82, Aeroflot's once-a-week flight into Washington's Dulles International Airport (a flight now not operating because of the cancellation of its rights) strayed off course sixteen times. In one of its more daring floutings of the rules in order to take photographs, Aeroflot Flight 315 en route to Dulles on November 8, 1981, diverted without authority over Pease Air Force Base near Plattsburgh, N.Y., and over other sensitive military installations. On its return flight, the same aircraft repeated the unauthorized route northbound. In retaliation the Soviets got a two-flight suspension. Another Aeroflot aircraft appeared over General Dynamics Electric Boat Division installations at Groton, Connecticut, at the very moment the first Trident nuclear submarine was being launched.

Since Aeroflot and the airlines of Soviet satellites carry out photographic espionage as part of the "game," it follows that the Soviets would believe that the South Koreans, Americans and others who fly into their sensitive territory would do exactly the same thing.

However, there is no evidence whatsoever that they do. Moreover, since the United States' super satellites give the Americans everything they need to know, why should they bother?

The Soviets' third charge was that the 747 was conducting electronic espionage by picking up signals from Soviet transmitters and radars monitoring ballistic missile testing and other activities that night and was retransmitting them to the American RC-135 by bursts of "coded electronic signals."

A standard Boeing 747 is capable of obtaining electronic intelligence – ELINT – by tuning its ultra-high-frequency radio to the appropriate military frequencies. A tape recorder, whether the cockpit voice recorder, or some other, would register the radio sound, which could include digital Soviet transmissions. A cockpit voice recorder contains only the last thirty minutes of cockpit sound, but other independent recording machines could be utilized.

On the other hand, again, why bother? The American RC-135's are on station twenty-four hours a day, at high altitude, close in to the Kamchatka Peninsula, where the international waters begin only twelve miles out from the shoreline. These aircraft could pick up any radio signals, whether digital, voice, or whatever, in the Kamchatka Peninsula area. If necessary, they or the E4's (adapted 747's) could be stationed over international waters in the Sea of Japan just to the south of Sakhalin Island to perform the same task.

It is therefore not possible to believe that Flight 007 was on a "spying" mission, if only for the reason that there would be no point to it. There is another reason: it is not possible to believe that an agency of the American government – in this case, as the Soviets allege, the CIA – would put the lives of 269 innocent civilians at risk to obtain information and intelligence readily available by other means.

On the other hand, circumstances in the Soviet Union did conspire to convince the Soviets, within the two hour and thirty-six minute time window, that the aircraft was in fact on an espionage mission. It is now known that, on that very night, the Soviets were undertaking testing, in the Kamchatka area, of their new intercontinental ballistic missile, the PL-5. The coincidence of that testing and the appearance of the intruder blip on the Kamchatka radar screen could readily convince the Soviet ADF commander at Biya and his paranoid staff that this was indeed an American spy aircraft (an RC-135 or a modified Boeing 747, the E4A or B) on a kamikaze mission to steal the telemetry and other information being transmitted by rocket and other equipment during the testing.

That was not the reason why the intruder was in Soviet airspace. It was not on a spying mission.

Was Flight 007 off course because of hijacking or unlawful interference? The ICAO report deals briefly and satisfactorily with the question of hijacking or "unlawful interference":

> There were 244 passengers on board from New York to Anchorage. Prior to departing New York, all passengers and their cabin luggage were security checked in accordance with FAA procedures. Four passengers stayed in Anchorage, the remainder waited in the transit/departure lounge during the turn-around. Two members of the New York-Anchorage cabin crew, who had special security training and responsibilities, remained on board the aircraft until relieved by the Anchorage-Seoul cabin crew. KAL procedures required the flight deck door to be locked during flight. It was unlocked by the flight crew only on request by the cabin staff and with the approval of the pilot-in-command. There was no indication in the radio transmissions of KE 007 of tensions or of an abnormal security situation on board.

It should also be observed that the course the 747 was following was on or near the Great Circle Route from Anchorage direct to Seoul, its original destination in accordance with its flight plan. Had there been a hijacking, the normal pattern is for the hijacker to select a destination other than the one for which the aircraft was originally bound.

For these reasons it is not possible to believe that Flight 007 was hijacked as it departed Anchorage for Seoul or at any time during the flight.

Was Flight 007 taking a deliberate short-cut? Korean Air Lines pilots' reputation in the industry for jumping the line has already been reviewed, as has the pilots' and, indeed, the entire corporation's well-known reputation for aggressiveness. Captain Chun's individual aggressiveness and leadership qualities have also been discussed.

The idea of going direct from Anchorage to Seoul by the Great Circle Route in order to save 178 nautical miles, twenty minutes of flying time and $2,600 in operating costs has been denounced by airline pilots and others as utterly foolish and impossible, given the risks associated with transiting Soviet airspace over the sensitive Kamchatka Peninsula, Sea of Okhotsk and Sakhalin Island area. And, taken by itself, flying that route for that purpose – well, no one in his right mind would do it. The question is: were Captain Chun and his crew in their right minds when they did it? Or were their minds so influenced by over-all company policy and its objectives that they decided to make a try for it? Perhaps they had never done it before, but there is a first time for everything.

What was company operating policy at the time Captain Chun and his crew took their 747 out of Anchorage bound for Seoul in the early morning hours of September 1?

AS HAS already been noted, Korean Air Lines had lost some $47.8 million in total during the operating years 1980-81. For an airline operating a forty-one aircraft fleet, those losses were staggering and had to be reversed. Aggressive cost-cutting steps had to be taken. In the words of KAL's chairman and president, Choong Hoon Cho, as set out in the company's annual report for 1981:

> Major steps taken during 1981 to improve our operating performance can be summarized as follows:
> - All-out efforts were made to maximize our operating revenues through enhancement of unit revenue by realigning our over-all marketing activities.
> - Intensive re-examination and analysis of expense-incurring factors were made in order to minimize overhead expenses.

As a result of taking these major steps, the company was

turned around and, in 1982, made a profit of $6 million. This was the result of hard-driving, aggressive cost-cutting done *"in order to minimize overhead expenses."*

The first place to which an airline must turn when considering cost-cutting is to its air operations. How can they be trimmed? How can fuel be saved? How can time in the air be cut?

A Boeing 747 costs on the average some $8,000 an hour to operate or about $130 a minute. That's what every minute saved from a programmed flight-planned flying time is worth. The scheduled block-to-block time for the Anchorage-Seoul run that night was eight hours twenty minutes, whereas, due to a lighter headwind than usual, the flight time on the computer flight plan was seven hours fifty-three minutes. If the flight could be done in only seven hours *thirty*-three minutes by going Anchorage-Seoul direct, the saving to the company would be approximately $2,600. As a matter of company policy, if out of the 130 international flights it operated each week, one hundred minutes a day were saved throughout the system, the value to the company would be in the range of $4 million a year. Even if the time saving was only twenty minutes a day, the money saving would be close to a million dollars a year, a highly respectable saving for a company trying to survive.

As a matter of company policy there could be incentive bonuses to those captains and crews that cut corners, jumped lines and saved the company money. A bonus of 50 per cent of the saving would not be unreasonable, but perhaps one-third of the saving might be what a prudent, cost-cutting company would offer.

There has been no admission by KAL that it has this sort of policy for pilots. It is, however, not unreasonable in the circumstances to assume that an incentive policy existed as of August 31, 1983. It would not, however, be company policy to approve of or countenance a "short-cut" across Soviet airspace.

Assuming it was company policy to cut corners in flying time without risk to its passengers, but with appropriate rewards to its pilots, it follows that Captain Chun, an aggressive and senior pilot in the KAL system – and a leader – would naturally want to set the pace and an example. He would also want to be entitled to any money or any other incentive the company offered for flight-time cutting.

Furthermore, he would know that the reputation of the Soviet interceptors, the Su-15's and MiG-23's, in the Kamchatka-Sakhalin area was poor and the chances of their catching him were slim. Anyway, if they did catch him he would have his running lights on. They would see that he was a civilian airliner and simply escort him on his way. They might have had a shot at Kim Chang Kyu back in 1978, but they wouldn't do that again even if they did intercept him. It couldn't happen to Captain Chun.

He knew that if he went down route R20 as he had flight-planned, he would have to pass through the Japanese civilian radar at Jyobonzan connected to Narita at Tokyo. But Narita air traffic control would probably accept his position reports at Noho, Inkfish, Matsushima and Niigata without checking him on the radar. That meant that he could fly the Great Circle Route from Anchorage to Seoul, over Sakhalin and close to the Siberian coast, and thereby stay out of the range of Japanese civilian surveillance radar at the southwest corner of Hokkaido at Yokotsudake.

In other words, he would do the direct run to Seoul, "cutting the corner," and give his radio reports for the waypoints without going through a civilian radar net to which he would have to report. He would leave his transponder on. Ordinarily the transponder would send an identification signal along with the plane's altitude back to the radar screen, where it would appear next to the blip of his aircraft. Even if it showed on the Japanese military radar scopes at Wakkanai, the observers would think he was Russian because he would be so far inside Soviet airspace.

So he probably wouldn't be caught by the civilian air traffic controllers as he cut his corner. He would give them the required waypoint reports all the way from Anchorage to

Seoul, even though he would be as much as three hundred miles off his flight-planned route.

If he took the short-cut he would be on the ground in Seoul twenty minutes before customs and baggage handling facilities were available. But he would just taxi up to the usual gate where the KAL company people would be waiting to guide him in. He would simply shut down and keep the passengers in the airplane until six o'clock.

THE JUDGMENT THAT Captain Chun was "cutting the corner" has been reinforced by ruthless after-the-event action taken by Korean Air Lines management as a result of Flight 007's being shot down.

It was reported by Associated Press that on Friday, February 17, 1984, a Korean Air Lines official had confirmed – "admitted" might be a better word – that KAL had shifted at least ten veteran pilots to ground duties.

The change of duties was part of disciplinary action begun after the Flight 007 incident and stepped up after a KAL DC-10 cargo jet collided with a twelve-seat Piper Navajo at Anchorage International Airport in December.

An unnamed KAL official said, "A reforming program has been enforced against pilots, co-pilots and flight engineers and some of them have been replaced by qualified juniors."

There must have been substantial cause and full evidence concerning the Flight 007 matter for KAL to take such drastic action against one of its veteran pilots, let alone ten of them. The same principle applies to the Anchorage DC-10 accident, which led to the dismissal of two senior pilots and the demotion of several others.

Dealing with KAL's disciplinary action following the Flight 007 disaster, the question is: Why did the air line take such a harsh step in grounding "at least ten veteran pilots?"

Obviously, KAL mounted a thorough internal investigation immediately after the event. Its investigating team would have at the top of its priority list a thorough examination of the records of all recent flights from Anchorage to Seoul over Route R20 prior to September 1, 1983. The reason? To find out whether there was any evidence that Captain Chun or any of his fellow captains had "cut the corner" across Soviet territory. If that wasn't the principal objective of the KAL investigators then why bother investigating?

What the KAL team found will probably never be disclosed. However, the harsh disciplinary action which was taken against such a large number of veteran pilots is clear evidence that they had been found guilty not of some sort of sporadic negligence but of illegal flight activities or deliberate rule violations of such magnitude as to justify the maximum disciplinary penalty that could be used against a pilot – grounding.

This is the very penalty that could have been imposed on Captain Chun if he had survived or gotten away with his corner cutting but was later found out.

Furthermore, if Captain Chun had gotten away with it, the Soviets certainly would not have made it known to the rest of the world that its vaunted Air Defense Forces were so ineffective that they failed to catch Flight 007.

By the same token, the Soviets would never admit that they had failed to intercept *any* KAL 747's that had taken the Anchorage-Seoul shortcut through Soviet airspace before September 1, 1983.

The answer to the question "Had KAL's 747's used from time to time the Anchorage-Seoul shortcut before the Flight 007 incident?" is found in the depth and severity of the disciplinary action taken against at least ten veteran pilots. The investigation was caused by the Flight 007 affair. The causal links between Flight 007's presence over Soviet territory, the investigation and the grounding of the pilots are direct and impossible to ignore.

There may be some other explanation as to why Captain Chun and his crew flew into Soviet airspace en route direct to Seoul. However, in the permanent absence of the black boxes, which might suggest some different explanation, all the evidence points to an attempt to "cut the corner." The famous San Francisco lawyer, Melvin Belli, who is acting for a relative of one of the victims, claims that he has witnesses who will give evidence in support of the corner-cutting proposition. Whether he does or not and can prove it in court remains to be seen.

Whatever the reason for Flight 007's being off course and in Soviet airspace, and whatever the grounds for the Soviets believing the intruder was on an electronic espionage mission for the United States, the shooting down of a civilian airliner has no justification in human, moral or civilized terms. All nations, including the United Nations and other relevant agencies, should create absolute safeguards to prevent a repeat of the 747 massacre.

If that proposition correctly states the case, then it is troubling to learn that in late 1983 a cache of SAMs (surface-to-air missiles) was installed near the White House to guard the President and his headquarters from surprise air attack. The word is that the security officers in control of the missiles from a command center in the Old Executive Office Building adjacent to the White House would have less than a minute to decide to fire if a plane deviated suspiciously from its flight pattern into or out of the nearby National Airport.

The result is that there could be a Flight 007-style massacre right over the heart of democracy in the western world, the White House.

Obviously, the Soviets have no monopoly on paranoia.

PIERS PAUL READ

THE TRAIN ROBBERS

On Thursday, August 8 1963, fifteen masked men stopped the night train from Glasgow to London and robbed it of £2,500,000. It was called the crime of the century, and the thieves were relentlessly pursued by Scotland Yard until half the gang were behind bars serving huge prison terms. But the story did not end there. First one, then another escaped in thrilling style and fled abroad, catching the world's imagination and making the Train Robbers into folk heroes.

Thirteen years later the gang combined to tell their story, and Piers Paul Read, author of the bestselling ALIVE, agreed to write it. Here in his brilliant hands is the complete and exclusive story of the century's most audacious crime and its even more sensational aftermath.

POST A LITTLE HAPPINESS

Post·A·Book

A Royal Mail service in association with the Book Marketing Council & The Booksellers Association.

Post-A-Book is a Post Office trademark.

STEPHEN FAY

THE GREAT SILVER BUBBLE

Early in 1980 the financial institutions of the western world teetered on the edge of panic as the price of silver went mad. Why did this happen? Who was responsible?

Behind the hysteria was a daring attempt by the royal family of Saudi Arabia and the Hunts of Texas to corner the silver market. Stephen Fay explains how they planned their coup, how they eventually failed, who stopped them and why it could happen again.

This is a story of intrigue and speculation, of greed and fear, and most of the participants would prefer that it was not told. THE GREAT SILVER BUBBLE reads like a novel with characters out of DALLAS – and it is all true.

CORONET BOOKS

IVAN FALLON AND JAMES SRODES

DELOREAN

John Zachary DeLorean is one of the most fascinating figures ever to enter the world of big money and international celebrity. With little more than his own forceful personality he created a business empire that controlled £250 million of other people's money and a 130 mph stainless steel gull-wing sports car which was to be his lasting memorial.

For two full years before his downfall, respected financial writers Fallon and Srodes tracked every move he made. Now they reveal the full story first hand – from his rise out of poverty to the top of General Motors – to the million dollar cocaine deal which sent his fantasy world crashing down around him. The result is one of the most intriguing dramas of our time.

CORONET BOOKS

FOX BUTTERFIELD

CHINA ALIVE IN THE BITTER SEA

In this unique and fascinating book, the western myths about modern China are shattered. Through first-hand reporting and personal interviews Fox Butterfield has captured the life of the Chinese as it is lived today. He examines the role of the Communist Party, its bureaucracy and its elite, and the grinding daily lives of the majority of the population. He discusses the impact of the Cultural Revolution and its implications for the future. Affectionate, accurate and brilliantly observed, CHINA: ALIVE IN THE BITTER SEA gives the reader one of the most comprehensive pictures of modern China ever written.

CORONET BOOKS

ANDREW BOYLE

THE CLIMATE OF TREASON

Andrew Boyle reveals how Burgess, Maclean and Philby were recruited by the Communist Party while undergraduates at Cambridge in the 1930s. They were the extreme cases, the men who actually spied against their country, but they were only the tip of the iceberg at a time when many members of the English upper class were active members.

In making his detailed researches Andrew Boyle uncovered other secret agents: 'Maurice', now revealed as Anthony Blunt and the mysterious 'Basil', the 'fifth' man recruited by the Russians to work in Washington. This revised and updated edition will remain the general reader's definitive account of one of the greatest of all espionage mysteries.

CORONET BOOKS

ALSO AVAILABLE FROM CORONET

PIERS PAUL READ
☐ 23779 1 The Train Robbers   £2.50

STEPHEN FAY
☐ 33033 3 The Greal Silver Bubble   £2.50

IVAN FALLON AND JAMES SRODES
☐ 35176 4 Delorean   £2.95

FOX BUTTERFIELD
☐ 33915 2 China Alive In The Bitter Sea   £4.50

ANDREW BOYLE
☐ 25572 2 The Climate Of Treason   £1.95

All these books are available at your local bookshop or newsagent, or can be ordered direct from the publisher. Just tick the titles you want and fill in the form below.

Prices and availability subject to change without notice.

CORONET BOOKS, P.O. Box 11, Falmouth, Cornwall.

Please send cheque or postal order, and allow the following for postage and packing:

U.K. – 50p for one book, plus 20p for the second book, and 14p for each additional book ordered up to a £1.68 maximum.

B.F.P.O. and EIRE – 50p for the first book, plus 20p for the second book, and 14p per copy for the next 7 books, 8p per book thereafter.

OTHER OVERSEAS CUSTOMERS – 75p for the first book, plus 21p per copy for each additional book.

Name ....

Address..

....